It's Not Too Late

How God Rescues Broken Relationships

Joyce C. Stanley

ISBN 978-1-64140-688-8 (paperback)
ISBN 978-1-64140-689-5 (digital)

Christian Faith Publishing, Inc.
832 Park Avenue
Meadville, PA 16335
www.christianfaithpublishing.com

Unless otherwise indicated, all Scripture quotations are from The ESV® Bible (The Holy Bible, English Standard Version®), copyright © 2001 by Crossway, a publishing ministry of Good News Publishers. Used by permission. All rights reserved.

Scripture quotations marked (NKJV) are from the New King James Version, copyright © 1979, 1980, 1982 by Thomas Nelson, Inc. Used by permission. All rights reserved.

Printed in the United States of America

Through her years of studying scripture and personal obedience to the will of God, Joyce Stanley led me to an understanding of what it means to truly be filled with the Holy Spirit. She patiently taught me the truth of the gospel and together we discovered the purpose God has for my life. Through her mentoring and wise counsel, I learned that God was more interested in changing my heart than my circumstances, and I eventually surrendered my desire to fix and change others, so they could meet my expectations. I have been set free from the lies that paralyzed me, and now I share the truth of God's redeeming love and grace with all who cross my path.

Midge Davis, VP and Former COO, Barrios Technology

Through Joyce's ministry I had a life changing experience with God. My faith, trust, and love for God grew. I learned how to truly forgive others, to forgive myself, and listen to God.

Dianna Hebert, Houston, Texas

I can't say enough about Joyce Stanley. She is a vessel used by God to bring amazing change to people who are hurting. God changed my life through her, bringing me from a person who was in the pit of despair, struggling with major depression, to someone with true joy. She taught me what the meaning of life is and how to have victory over life's mess. Christ is, and always will be, the answer to whatever we are going through. Joyce is an authority on how to go about doing this in your own life.

Stacy Janis, Houston, Texas

Contents

Prologue 7

1   Sara's Story—Thirty-Three Years Earlier....................15

2   Nick's Story—Thirty-Six Years Earlier 26

3   The Yellow-Haired Girl in the Red Parka...................33

4   Migraine Headaches..40

5   The Breakfast Meeting..50

6   The Counseling Process...56

7   The Fruit of Brokenness...66

8   My Husband Is My Father? 75

9   It's Nick's Turn 84

10   Sara's Sister, Jane..99

11   A New Career...111

12   Andrea's Story—Ten Years Earlier 112

13   Proclaim Recovery..131

14   Set Free 146

Epilogue 153

Appendix A 155

Appendix B 165

Appendix C 183

Prologue

The End of a Marriage

Sara jumped at Nick's abrupt tap on her shoulder. She had been mindlessly watching the eggs sizzle and the butter splatter over the once-gleaming stainless steel cook top. Sara awoke from her daydream and spun around to see Nick standing before her. Her eyes widened as she fixed them on the suitcase sitting in front of the dishwasher. The warmth of the sun-drenched morning instantaneously changed to a coldness as a shiver went through her body.

"I'm leaving, and I don't want you to try to stop me," Nick said in a hushed voice. "I don't want the kids to know."

"What do you mean, you're leaving? I thought things were getting better," she said, her legs buckling. She was shaking like a leaf.

"I'm tired of everything. Nothing is changing. You're no different. I'm just going through the motions for the kids' sake. I need to be somewhere by myself."

Sara opened her mouth, but her words stopped at the back of her throat. Her stomach churned, and she wanted to run before she got sick. Her face hardened, jaw locked, and her eyes brimmed with tears. She fought them, closed her eyes, and stifled her scream.

Nick pivoted on his heel, grabbed his suitcase, and hurried out of the kitchen. Their two teenagers sauntered down the hallway, backpacks in hand, hair combed, and ready for middle school.

"Hey, Dad, where you going? On a trip?" Madison shouted as Nick let the storm door slam behind him. He always said good-bye, but this morning was different.

"Your breakfast is in the pan," Sara whispered as the kids walked toward her. "I need to get dressed."

Sara closed the bathroom door and sank to the floor, grasping her knees with her locked fingers. She was numb, but her mouth opened and stretched so widely that she thought her head would explode. A silent scream squeaked into the air.

"I don't understand. I just don't understand. What am I going to do now? What should I tell the kids?" Sara clutched her knees, rocked back and forth on her haunches, and dropped her head onto her knees.

Nick and Sara were childhood sweethearts, married immediately following college graduation, and spent every free moment together in the early years. Now, after fifteen years of marriage, conversation was cold and rare, as Sara enjoyed time with the kids, Madison and Michael, rather than Nick. He spent more time at work and constantly found reasons not to come home when she was there. For the last year, Sara wondered if they were going to make it and why she was so unhappy.

The knocking on the door persisted as Sara braced her back against it. She had to gather her wits about her and pay attention to Michael's calls.

"Mom, what are you doing? Are you okay? We need to leave, so can you come out and say good-bye?"

Wiping her eyes on her robe's sleeve, Sara found a Kleenex and blew her nose. As she weakly pushed herself up, she stood, opened the door, and faced her son.

"What's up, Mom? Are you sick? We need to go—we have tests today."

"No, I'm fine. You guys hurry or you'll miss your bus. I'll see you tonight."

She walked the fraternal twins to the front door, hugged them both, and watched them sprint onto the school bus. She had faithfully performed this ritual almost every day of their school lives, so she could provide the stability at home for them as Nick traveled the state as a regional manager for a major corporation. Sara and Nick had agreed to her role with the twins so that Nick could concentrate on his career.

At least the kids seem to be all right, for today anyway. What did Nick mean, that he needs to be alone somewhere? Where is he going? Is he by himself, or is he with another woman?

Dark thoughts swirled in her mind, and the more she thought about Nick and what he said, the more her hands shook and her lips quivered. Everything she thought was stable was out of control, and she couldn't get a handle on anything—what to do, where to go, whom to call. The tomb of her home closed in around her. She poured some coffee to calm her nerves, and she called her best friend, Emma, who lived next door.

"Hello," Emma said. There was no response from the other end.

Sara whimpered and then sobbed uncontrollably. "Oh, Emma, Nick's left me, and I don't know what to do."

"Let me get the baby and gather up his things. I'll be there as fast as I can."

After what seemed like an eternity, the doorbell rang. Sara pulled herself up from the kitchen table and walked dazed to the front door. Disheveled and with eyes red and puffy, she greeted Emma.

"Come on in," she said in a barely audible whisper.

Emma wrapped one arm around Sara's shoulder, as she held baby Collin with her other arm. "I came as fast as I could. What happened?"

"I don't know. Nick just got up this morning and said he was leaving and not to try to stop him."

Sara and Emma walked into the living room and sat down on the down-filled sofa cushions. Sara had slept there many nights when she and Nick were fighting. It was her way of getting away from the arguing, although morning never brought resolution, just silence. In the last several years the conflict had intensified, and now in this last year there were long periods of deafening silence. She often felt the coldness and distance when Nick came into the room. Sara knew they had problems, but she didn't know how to fix them. She got busier with the twins, and Nick didn't seem to need her anymore. His job became more demanding, and their lives were two trains traveling on separate tracks. Today, those trains collided.

"Here, Collin, here's your bottle," Emma said, laying her nine-month-old son on his soft blanket on the floor before her. She wanted him to take his nap so she could console her friend.

"What can I do to help you?" she said as she turned toward Sara.

"I don't know. I feel like I've been hit in the stomach and I'm going to throw up. I don't know where Nick is or when or if he's coming back. He said he needs to be by himself. Where does that leave me and the twins?"

"I'm so sorry. I have a friend who's a divorce attorney. Do you want me to call him?"

"No, I don't want to start there, yet. I don't know what to do, but I know I don't want a divorce. I guess I shouldn't have been so stubborn when Nick wanted us to get counseling. I thought we could get better by ourselves. The thought of counseling always made me think I must be sick or something."

"Do you think Nick might have found someone else?"

"Oh, no, I really can't go there. But, I must admit I've wondered about that recently when things just seemed to be getting worse. I don't know if I could ever know the truth if I asked him. He wants to be alone. I guess that means not only without me, but without the kids, too. I don't have any answers, for me or them. Oh, Emma, what can I tell them about their father?"

"For right now, just let them think that he's on a business trip. They're in the middle of finals, and they really don't need to be upset. You'll have to tell them eventually, but not today. Why don't you let them come to my house after school today? They can study, and you can rest."

"I don't need rest. I need to know what I'm going to do."

"You really won't know anything until you hear from Nick."

"I think he's on a path to say goodbye to his family. I need to find out what path I need to be on."

Mamma mia, here I go again—Sara's mobile phone rang out with the old ABBA song. It was her mother calling.

"Oh, no, what should I tell her?"

"I don't know. It's your decision."

Sara didn't want to lie to her mother and have it come back to bite her. Her voice shook as she answered the phone.

"Hello," she said timidly. "Mom, I really can't talk right now. I have a friend here, and she'll be leaving soon. Can I call you back?"

"You sound sick. Are you okay?"

"Yes," said Sara. "I was taking a nap when my friend came over, so I'm not fully awake yet. I'll talk to you later."

"I hope that satisfies her, at least for a while. I can't deal with her and her questions right now," Sara said as she turned to her friend.

Emma was pouring herself a cup of steaming coffee, and as she put it down to cool, she said, "Tell me what's been going on. I know things have been difficult, but Nick leaving? How long have things been rough?"

"I guess for a couple of years, if I'm honest about it. We really don't talk, just about decisions we have to make about the kids. We stopped going out a long time ago, and we never have friends in anymore. You're the only friend I talk to, and the rest of the time I spend with the kids. I guess they've become my outlet, now that they're getting older, and we can do things together. I think the problems have been simmering under the surface for a while, and I was hoping they would get better, or just go away if we were committed to the kids. I never thought Nick would leave or want a divorce. I didn't think it was in him to do that. I thought when we started going to church, that would solve everything, but it didn't."

Picking up her cup and holding it in her two hands to her lips, her friend said, "I'm no marriage counselor, but I do know this. Problems just don't go away by themselves. They stay buried inside us until one day they come out in some way, usually in an explosion. That's what used to happen in our house. That's why I try really hard to talk things through when I sense that there's something wrong."

"But, how do you know when something is wrong or you've offended someone? I could be apologizing all day long, because I never seem to do anything right in Nick's eyes. He frowns at me a lot and rolls his eyes to tell me he disapproves. I'm walking on eggshells with him, and so I just stop talking, because whatever I say, I'll be wrong."

"Wow, that's hard. I'm lucky that I can talk to Jim, but it wasn't always that way. We've really had to work at it. We decided a long time ago that divorce was not an option, and that living miserably with each other wasn't either. So, our only option was to talk it out, to work it out. We didn't get there by ourselves, though. We've had help."

"What kind of help?" said Sara.

"Our first year of marriage was a nightmare. Two self-centered people all of a sudden living in the same house. We both had been single and on our own for a long time, and, here we were supposed to put the other person's needs before our own. We didn't know how to do that. Each of us wanted our own way and that led to a lot of fighting. We wanted children and didn't want to bring them into a home of arguing. We had had some premarital counseling, but it really didn't prepare us for marriage. Thankfully, a friend recommended a counselor who really helped us. It wasn't easy, but I'm sure glad we did it."

"How long ago was that, and do you think counseling could help me? I don't know if Nick would go. He wanted us to get help a long time ago, but it might be too late."

"One thing I do know is that a person has to want to get help. In our case, both Jim and I wanted to learn and change. Maybe it was because we were older and committed not to divorce, I don't know. But, a wife can't change her husband or force him to go to a counselor. Nick has to want that for himself, and so must you."

"All I know is that I don't want a divorce, and I don't want to lose my husband and kids. If I need to get help, then so be it. Right now, I think Nick is just so angry. I don't know if it would work with him."

"That doesn't matter. If you're ready to get help, then you be the one. You can't fix your marriage, or Nick, but you can deal with you. One thing our counselor taught us is that in a marriage relationship, one person usually wants the other to change first. We can't make that happen. We can only be responsible for ourselves."

Collin started to whimper, and he opened his striking blue eyes. Emma had almost forgotten about him. He had been so quiet and peaceful as he slept. He was such a good baby, the youngest in a string of five siblings.

"Just think, Sara, I could've missed all this. I have to believe there's hope for you and Nick. Do you mind if I pray for you and ask my church to pray for you and your family?"

"No, I would appreciate it," said Sara. "Please pray—and where can I find the name of a counselor? In the phone book?"

"Hold on," said Emma. "Let me check. I don't know if the person we saw is still here, but I'll see if I can get some recommendations. You need to see someone with good references, not just pick anyone out of a telephone book or off the Internet."

Emma picked up Collin and held him closely. He contentedly rested his head on her chest. "I need to go, but I will call you as soon as I can have a name for you. And, remember, I will be praying for you."

Sara looked down as her friend spoke. No one had ever offered to pray for her, and she didn't know how to respond. Her insides tightened with anxiety, but Emma was a friend, and Sara trusted her.

"Thanks," Sara said sheepishly. "I'll wait for your call. I'll be home all day."

Sara lay on the couch to rest. This was the worst morning of her life.

1

Sara's Story—Thirty-Three Years Earlier

Sara heard the doorbell ring and ran to answer it. Opening the metal screen door, she saw Alan, her neighborhood friend. They were in the first grade at Shady Elementary School, and today was a sunny day in a summer that had been especially dreary and rainy.

"Can you come out and play?" said Alan. "I brought my scooter."

Alan's shiny silver scooter lay on its side on the sidewalk. Alan was chubby, and the other boys in their class didn't play with him. He didn't run fast and play soccer as well as some of the others. When they teased him, Sara defended him and played with him instead of the girls. They had become fast friends.

"Sure. Let me go get mine."

Sara ran back into the house, grabbed her scooter from the hall closet, opened the screen door, and slammed it behind her. She didn't ask permission to leave.

Sara was the youngest in a family with four children. By the time she was six, her sister was already nineteen and working outside the home. Her brothers were ten and fifteen years old, and she often had no interaction with them for days. At the age of six, she was on her own most of the time.

Dad was self-employed, worked long hours, and Sara didn't see him very much, if at all. Mother was overwhelmed with her responsibilities. She functioned as her husband's secretary, answered the phone, and soothed impatient customers. Sara didn't catch any spare minutes of attention on the average day. She took care of herself.

Sara sat down beside Alan on her front concrete stoop. The house was a small brick ranch style, the only brick home on a block of wood siding homes. It was a mark of success, the fact that her dad had built a brick house on their street, a middle-class neighborhood of hardworking families.

"Can I try your scooter?" she said to her friend. "I think it is faster than mine."

"Sure. Can you ride it to my house?"

"Okay," said Sara.

Alan's home was around the corner from hers, and their backyards connected. It seemed like a long way away, but she went where she wanted. She often played all day and came back home at dinnertime. Today was Saturday, and it was good to be outside.

The two friends got up from the stoop, mounted their scooters, and took off down the sidewalk, while they maneuvered the cracks and raised up concrete with tree roots looking for an escape. As they reached Alan's house, Sara looked up and saw the massive, looming, white wooden house. She had not been inside because she and Alan always played in his backyard. It was so big compared to her home. It had at least three stories, or so she thought.

"Is there anyone home with you?" said Sara. "I don't think I want to go in. Your house looks scary."

"My mom and dad and my big brother," said Alan. "You'll be okay."

Sara had never met or seen his family. Her parents weren't friends with them, but her parents weren't friends with any of their neighbors. There was no time for that.

They removed their skates on the expansive gray painted front porch, and Sara followed Alan into the house.

"Just follow me," he said, as they walked down the dark, wood-paneled hallway.

Mr. and Mrs. Butler were sitting at the kitchen table as the two children cautiously entered the room.

"Is it okay if I brought a friend over?" Alan said to his mom.

Mrs. Butler looked up from her coffee and morning paper and grimaced at her son. "Who's this?"

"It's Sara," said Alan. "She lives down the street and around the corner. She's in my class."

"I suppose so," said his mother. "What are you going to do? I don't really want you in the house. Your brother is still sleeping."

Alan's brother David slept late in the mornings. He didn't go to school anymore and was home a lot. He was sixteen.

The children passed through the kitchen, opened the wooden screen door, and stepped out onto the back porch. There was no air-conditioning, so the doors and windows stayed open to cool the house. Sara could hear the whirring of the window fans in the upstairs bedrooms. The torn screen caught her shirt as it closed.

Unhooking her shirt from the screen, Sara said, "Okay, what should we do now? Do you want to play Marco Polo? I'll be Marco." Sara tagged Alan and bounded down the porch steps.

"Wait, I didn't say go yet!" Alan shouted.

Sara always won at tag, because Alan couldn't run as fast as she, and she knew it. Alan made a face, because she was already running into the yard before he could reach the bottom of the steps. Tag was not his favorite game because he always lost. He liked games like checkers, which allowed him to sit. At least he had a chance to win. Alan was smart and quick—just not on his feet. But he decided to do what Sara wanted, since she was one of his few friends.

The next Saturday, it wasn't hard for Sara to recruit some more neighborhood children to go with her to Alan's to play Marco Polo. She was affable and made friends easily. Alan's yard was the biggest one in the whole neighborhood, so the other children were eager to go with her.

"Come on, let's go," she said to the others as they cut through her backyard to Alan's yard. They could play without Mr. and Mrs. Butler knowing they were there.

"Marco! Polo!" Their voices rang out as they ran after each other with eyes closed.

Sara loved to run, but the other little boys were fast, too, and sometimes faster. There were no girls living on her street, just boys. Sara wanted a friend with whom she could play baby dolls, but there were none. To fit in, she learned to play tag games and hide-and-seek with the boys. Alan was "it" a lot.

A New Friend

"Hey, can I play, too?" said David, opening the back door and yelling at the top of his lungs.

"Aw, you don't want to play with us, do you?" said Alan.

"Sure," said David, as he closed the door behind him. His parents were not home, and he had been left "in charge" of his brother.

"What are you doing?" David asked Alan, Sara, and the other boys.

"We're playing hide-and-seek," they said. "Want to play?"

"Okay," said David. "You go hide, and I'll come find you." He ran to the closest tree, closed his eyes, and began to count. "One, two, three, four, five, six, seven, eight, nine, ten. Ready or not, here I come."

The children scattered and ran in all directions. The yard was so big that there was a myriad of places to hide—under bushes, behind trees, under the back porch.

"I found you!" David yelled as he uncovered a little one's den, and the giggles and delighted screams swept the neighborhood.

David became the children's new playmate. He taught them new games and was a fun friend. He was always home when Sara came to play with Alan.

One day as Sara ran through the lush, green grass, long arms scooped underneath her.

"I've got you," David said, as he grabbed her, perched her atop his shoulders, and settled her in behind his neck. Her six-year-old legs wrapped around him.

This was a new feeling for her, that of being favored by an older boy. She hardly ever saw her two brothers, and she didn't spend any time with her daddy. David's attention made her feel warm and giggly inside.

David ran with Sara throughout the yard and back to the house, pretending to be a horse with a rider. The other children looked on. Sara was having so much fun with David that she wanted to come back again to play with him. He carried her on his shoulders each time she came to Alan's yard.

"Do you want me to show you the playhouse I have built in our basement?" said David to Sara a few weeks later.

"Sure," she said, "do you have any toys in it?"

"I have lots of toys you might like."

The doors to the storm cellar opened into the yard, and David walked down the five dirty steps into the dank space. They were underground, and Sara smelled the mustiness and felt the dampness as David took her down from his shoulders. It was summer, but the basement was winter. Outside the golden sun had warmed her soft, pale skin, but here her insides chilled. Her bright red playsuit wasn't enough to keep her warm.

Clotheslines stretched across the room, and wet clothes hung from them like people. Metal chairs, a table with a broken leg, and a tool bench with rusted pieces of metal lived in this space with the clothes. Hunter green painted concrete walls completed the look of the unwelcoming room.

David took her by the hand and led her into a smaller room. It was even colder than the first.

"This is our fruit cellar. We store canned fruits and vegetables in here. I call it my playhouse. We can make up stories and put on plays here."

Sara shook as she stood in the cold storage space. She looked up and saw row after row of brightly colored Mason jars, filled with tomatoes, peppers, and peaches. The shelves stretched to the ceiling.

"I'm cold," she said. "Can we go back outside?"

"Let's play doctor," David said. "That will warm you up."

"Okay. Can I be the nurse?"

"No, you can be the patient whose mommy just brought her to the doctor. I'll be the doctor."

He picked her up and carried her to a glider whose sunny days on the front porch were long gone. There was no cushion, just rusty springs that once supported brightly flowered cushions. The Butlers hadn't watched the fireflies from that glider for years. Alan was the only one who came out of the house on a regular basis.

David laid her on the springs of the glider, its paint peeling mercilessly, and piled some rags under her head. She winced as she felt the hard springs hit her back. She was tiny and thin, and her back was bony. The springs pressed into her skin. Sara looked up and saw a lone light bulb hanging from the ceiling, and the yellowed brightness of it hurt her eyes.

"Let's play doctor," said David. "Do you like to play doctor?"

Sara shook her head, "Uh-huh."

David slid his sweaty hands under the small of her back. Stuffing spilled from a dirty cushion lying on the floor. He reached down, grabbed some filthy stuffing and pretended to pull it out from her body.

"See, Sara, Dr. David needs to fix you. I can make you all better."

Sara froze as she watched him pulling pieces of cotton from the floor. He lifted her clothes and placed his hands on her. She did not take her eyes off the light bulb, and eventually, she closed her eyes so she couldn't see. She didn't understand what was happening; David was her friend, a big brother.

When he was finished, he put her clothes on her and pulled her up.

"Wasn't that fun?" he said. "Are you all better now?"

Her back hurt from the springs, but she was too scared to speak.

David was in the yard each time she played with Alan, and inevitably, he would scoop her up and place her atop his shoulders. Her playtime with Alan and the other neighbor children would always end with David and her descending the steps to the underground cellar.

The wolf's den became the destination, and her captor became bolder and more brazen with her little body. The six-year-old didn't know what to do, and she feared she would be taken by David each time she stepped outside her house to play.

The Lost Friendship

"Can you come out to play?" Alan said, standing on the other side of the screen door.

"No," said Sara, "I can't."

"We haven't played together for a long time," Alan said. "I have some new games."

"That's okay. I need to stay home and help my mommy today."

Sara lied about the reason she couldn't play. She felt safer inside her own house, even though she didn't know why fear gripped her insides when Alan questioned her.

Mrs. Matheson passed behind Sara and overheard the youngsters' conversation.

"It's okay, Sara," she said. "You can go out and play with Alan."

Sara's heart filled with fear. "My tummy hurts, Mommy. I don't want to go." Another lie, but the fear that gripped her was powerful enough to make her stomach do somersaults.

"Come on inside, then, and let me give you something to make your tummy feel better. I'm sorry, Alan, Sara can't play right now."

He hung his head and turned on his heel and walked away.

Mommy took out some ginger ale, which Sara didn't like. "I think my tummy feels better," said Sara.

"Sara, does your tummy really hurt, or is there some reason you don't want to play with Alan? Don't you like him anymore? I thought he was your best friend."

There it was. This was her chance to tell Mommy about the cellar, but she didn't know what to say. David's words turned over and over in her mind.

"I'm your new big brother, and you're my little sister. Don't tell your mommy or your daddy, or even your brothers, about our doctor game. If you do, I'll tell them what a bad little girl you are, and you'll really be in trouble," David had said to her more than once. In fact, every time she was in their "playroom", he warned her of the consequence of her telling anyone about it.

Would she get a big spanking, or maybe not be allowed to play with anyone for a really long time? Sara tried to think about what her punishment could be if she told about David and her playing doctor. If it were just a game, why did her body feel so bad?

She stood and stared at her mother and tried to muster the courage to open her mouth.

"Sara, if you always tell me the truth, I won't get angry with you. But, if you lie to me, then I will know that I can't trust you. So tell me the truth, and everything will be all right." Her mother had told her this many times. They didn't have many teaching moments together, but this is one thing she hammered into Sara's psyche—always tell the truth. The episodes with David had scared her into doing what he told her to do. His words controlled her, but now her mother's promise gave her strength to tell her about David and the Butlers' storm cellar.

The Confession

"David and I have been playing doctor," Sara said sheepishly.

"David? David who?" said Sara's mother.

"Alan's big brother," said Sara.

Mrs. Matheson didn't know that Alan had a brother, because neither she nor her husband knew the family well.

"What do you mean, 'playing doctor?'"

"He has a playroom in his basement, and we play doctor."

Sara's family lived in a small town where sexual abuse was not commonly discussed. Mrs. Matheson had never told Sara not to let anyone touch her inappropriately, and she did not understand the magnitude of what Sara was telling her. She asked Sara no questions, and Sara didn't know how to put into words what had happened to her in that basement.

Sara was relieved that the secret was out, but she wondered what the punishment would be. She had been taught in church that she must always do the right thing, whatever that meant. Sara walked away from her mother and waited for the punishment, because she now believed she could go to hell. She had no idea what was next, but she waited for something bad to happen.

The Confrontation

Sara sat in a chair against the wall in the crowded living room. Mr. and Mrs. Butler and David sat on the sofa. Mr. and Mrs. Matheson sat on chairs on opposite ends of the room. Their voices were muffled, and David muttered something she could not understand.

"We won't allow her to come to your house anymore," said Sara's father. "We'll block the opening at the end of our yard that she goes through to get to your yard."

Sara was an outsider, a fly on the wall watching this spectacle, but no one spoke to her or asked her anything. She felt guilty; it was her fault—the playtimes, the playing doctor, everything. Mr. and Mrs. Butler stared at her and got up and walked to the front door with David. The fathers shook hands, and the family that lived behind them exited their home. It was the first and last time they crossed the threshold of the Matheson home.

With no explanation, no discussion, Mrs. Matheson said, "Sara, go to your room and get ready for bed."

Sara stoically walked from the living room, down the hallway, and into her bedroom. She mechanically got her nightgown from under her pillow and dressed for bed.

What just happened? Was everyone mad at me? Was everything my fault?

Sara crawled into her bed and pulled the covers over her head. It was a big bedroom she shared with her older sister, who was hardly ever home. Sara always felt lost in it and alone. The meeting in their living room with the Butlers made her room not a place of comfort, but of condemnation. A large wooden crucifix hung above her bed, and Sara hid from it.

"God is mad at me, too."

The next morning, after a fitful night's sleep, Sara awoke to her mother's call to breakfast—the daily bowl of sticky oatmeal waited for her on the table. This was her fare every morning, and each day, Sara tried to gag the hated stuff down her throat. Today, breakfast was especially difficult.

"Sara, your father doesn't ever want you to play with Alan, and you are not allowed in his house or his yard," her mother said, as she watched her daughter push her cereal with her spoon.

Sara gulped, and the tears crept through her lashes. She tried to blink them away, but she thought her heart would break. She held her stomach, and looking at the cold oatmeal made her feel worse.

"Why? Alan is my best friend. He didn't do anything. I won't be able to play with him—ever?"

"There's nothing I can do. Those are your father's orders, and if you disobey, he'll be really mad and take out his belt."

Because Sara feared her father, his gruff voice, and especially 'the belt,' she never played with Alan again, either at his house or in his yard. The friends ended their friendship, and no one said the name "David" in her home from that day forward. It was as if he didn't exist, neither he nor his family. Sara's parents never spoke of the meeting, the sexual abuse, or asked Sara any questions. That was not a conversation the Mathesons would ever have with her. Sara was left, at the tender and vulnerable age of six, to figure it out by herself.

That night, Sara turned off the light switch by her bedroom door, ran across the room, jumped into bed, and yanked the covers over her head. Afraid of the dark, she pulled her legs up to her chest so she lay in a fetal position. Her insides shook as she saw behind her closed eyes a boy, a teenager on a motorcycle. It was David. He was intent on running her over, and she ran from street corner to street corner trying to escape. She attempted to cross the street to get to safety, but the motorcycle was after her with her every step. She kept running and running, trying to escape. The fear-filled chase mushroomed into a horrible nightmare, which started the evening David and his parents walked out of her house.

2

Nick's Story—Thirty-Six Years Earlier

"Nicholas, watch what you're doing!" yelled Nick's mother as a miniature metal truck hit her foot.

Stirring a pot of spaghetti sauce, she stood preparing dinner at the stove. She and Nick lived with her mother, "Mimi," because Nick's father was away in the war.

Accustomed to his mother's high-pitched and emotion-packed voice, Nick continued to look down at his trucks, scooting them along in his make-believe world. At two and a half, he lived in an upstairs apartment over a grocery store and listened to his grandmother and mother talk excitedly and incessantly.

"What the —— are you doing, kid?" said Uncle Henry as he set groceries down on the table. "Got those trucks again?"

Uncle Henry had no wife or children, and because he was legally blind, he had not been accepted into the army. He helped out when he could, but his capabilities were limited. He was not limited, however, in his knowledge of swear words and foul language. They tumbled from his mouth as easily as he said "hello."

Another truck slammed into Mrs. Antonio's foot. "Nicholas!" she said.

"Oh, ——," Nick said, repeating one of Uncle Henry's favorite expletives.

"What did you say?" his mother said. "I'm going to wash your mouth out with soap. I told you never to say that word again."

Nick looked up from his trucks. He often repeated words his uncle said, but he didn't know the difference between acceptable and unacceptable ones. People visiting the apartment often used language he shouldn't learn, and Uncle Henry was the biggest offender. He was one of only two men in Nick's life right now; Poppy was the second one. All the other males in the family were overseas, including Nick's father.

Mrs. Antonio grabbed the bar of soap, put it in water to make it soapy, and grabbed Nick by the arm. She stuck the soap into his mouth, and he choked, coughed, and cried at the same time, swallowing the terrible-tasting stuff that hurt his mouth.

"That'll teach you not to say naughty words," said his mother.

Sobbing, Nick said nothing. Nick didn't talk much to anyone after that and climbed inside his world of make-believe trucks where he felt safe.

Homecoming

"Nick, this is your daddy," said Mrs. Antonio.

A tall, lanky man stood before him, dressed in a khaki army uniform, ribbons and medals hanging from his pocket. He stretched out his hands toward Nick, but the crying, frightened little boy clung to his mother and crawled up her chest to get away from his father.

"He's become very shy with people. I don't know why. He has a hard time talking, and he doesn't seem to want to go to anyone except me and my mother. Don't feel bad," she said, "it's not your fault. He doesn't know you at all. After all, he was born while you were deployed. I've looked forward to your coming home so you could help me with him."

The "help" that Mrs. Antonio had anticipated never came, because her husband quickly found a job, which required long hours.

"Why can't you get a job where you can at least be home for dinner?" she said to her husband one evening, hours after Nick was asleep.

"I need to make money so we can move out of this apartment. I don't want to live with your parents for the rest of our lives. With so many vets coming home, I need to work as much as I can, or someone else will get my job."

Nick never got to know his father, because his job became the most important thing in his dad's life—not until he was a teenager when he could work for his father in his business. The relationship never became that of father and son. As a teenager, his relationship with his dad became employer-employee. He learned firsthand how important his dad's livelihood was to him.

The Delivery

"God, help me, please," said Nick as he tried turning the wheel of the truck in the direction of the skid.

Nick had just learned to drive the delivery van for the supermarket, which his dad owned in partnership with his brothers. The boxes of groceries slid and crashed into each other as Nick kept the van from sliding out of control. A new driver at the age of sixteen, he was expected to know how to drive in icy conditions. He was expected to know how to do everything associated with his after-school job.

Nick slowly maneuvered the gasping van up the hazardous driveway, and he looked up to see Mrs. Lorenzo in the window. He put the gearshift in park and walked around and opened the back doors. Her box of groceries was intact, and Nick heaved a sigh of relief. The glass bottles hadn't broken, for the fresh produce packed around them had cushioned them.

"Nick, I didn't expect you'd make it all the way up here on a night like tonight. A lot of businesses have closed early, I understand, because the roads are so bad."

"Not 'the store,' Mrs. Lorenzo," said Nick. "You know they never close. My dad says we have to take care of our customers."

"I know, Nick," she said. "Tell me, are you going to the championship game tomorrow night?"

His high school basketball team was vying for state championship, and it was their biggest game of the year.

"No, I have to work. It's a Friday night, and we have to get the orders delivered for the weekend," he said, as he looked down and away from her inquiring brown eyes.

Mrs. Lorenzo was nice to Nick, and she was one of the few people in his life who seemed to understand him. She never yelled or was short with him, and he genuinely liked her. She held out her hand and gave him a tip for his service, the only one he would get that whole weekend.

As Nick walked down the steep steps and climbed into the front seat of the van, he thought, *At least she cares whether or not I go to the game. My dad doesn't even know there's a game.*

After the last box of groceries was delivered, Nick inched the van into its space behind the store. He walked into the back storage room and hung the ignition keys on the hook on the board on the wall. Nick's dad came out from behind a stack of boxes.

"All done?" he said.

"Yes, sir," said Nick.

There was no reply. Nick wondered if he could get a ride home so he could do his homework. The hours of his after-school job were long, and they left little time for studying. Tomorrow he had a big test, and he didn't want to fail. He walked out into the store and tried to corral a ride.

The Future

"Nick, have you ever thought of going to college?" said Mrs. Lorenzo one day when Nick delivered her groceries.

"No, I don't think I'll have the grades, and besides, I don't think my parents can afford it."

"Well, have you ever thought about what you're going to do after you graduate from high school? Do you plan to work in a supermarket for the rest of your life?"

"I guess so. That's probably what my dad wants me to do. I haven't thought much about it, though."

"How are your grades?" said Mrs. Lorenzo.

"Not too great," said Nick. "I don't get much time to study because I work every day after school."

"Grades are important, but other things are important, too. Have you taken your SAT exam yet?"

"No," he said. "I passed it up last year, because college was not an option for me."

"If it would be okay with your parents, I could tutor you this year and help prepare you for them. As an English teacher, I've helped many students prepare for college."

Mrs. Lorenzo taught at the high school, but she taught the "smart kids," the ones who were in the honors classes. Nick made average to below average grades, and he never aspired to do better. Her offer to help him gave him confidence. Mom and Dad never spoke of college, grades, or Nick's future. They expected hard work from him at the store, and Nick didn't dream of anything else.

"Would you like me to talk to your dad about my tutoring proposition?"

"No," he said. "I'll do it. He'll probably say yes as long as I can get all the orders delivered."

"Good, then I'll expect you in my classroom tomorrow after school. Bring your willingness to learn."

"Thanks a lot, Mrs. Lorenzo. I really appreciate that. I'll talk to my dad, and I'm sure I'll be there after school. If he says no, then I'll let you know I can't make it."

Nick whistled and practically ran down her front steps and jumped into the front seat of the van. The sun shone brighter and the air felt cleaner in the town today. Mrs. Lorenzo cared about him.

The Teacher and the Pupil

Nick was right. His father didn't care if he came to work a little late. He just had to complete the deliveries to the customers. Nick was determined to make it all work out. For the first time, he had hope in his heart that his future could be something more than the family's supermarket.

"Nick, come on in and sit down," said Mrs. Lorenzo.

Nick saw the stacks of books and the homework papers on her desk. "Are you sure you have the time to do this, to help me?" he said.

"Yes, Nick," she said. "You're a good kid, and I believe we can do this."

She opened a workbook and tore out a practice test. "Answer these questions. I need to know where to start."

Nick took a pencil from his backpack, sat down at the student's desk, and began to read the questions. He answered them, but many were guesses.

I hope she doesn't think I'm stupid, thought Nick as he handed her the test. *I know I need help.*

"Good job, Nick. Let me see where we are with this test."

That day began a teacher-pupil relationship built on trust and respect. By the end of that semester, Nick's grades had improved remarkably. He had never really studied before, and for the first time in his school life, someone was teaching him not only his subjects but also study habits. It was as if a light had come on inside him and was illuminating every day. He had a newfound purpose—to study, to get good grades, and to succeed. He began to believe that he could do it; he could go to college.

3

The Yellow-Haired Girl in the Red Parka

"Where do you go to school?" Sara asked, as they danced around the floor in the big, airy dance hall. She glanced up to see the sparkling lights beaming across the ceiling, reflected from the silver ball.

The disc jockey played the slow dance set that were Sara's favorite songs. It seemed to Sara that Nick wanted to dance with her for the whole night. Sara felt special and chosen, because this guy was definitely a college guy, and she had just graduated from high school.

"Oh, it's a small school. I'm too embarrassed to tell you the name, because I'm sure you've never heard of it," he said facetiously with a large grin flashing across his face. "It was the only school that would accept me."

"Oh, c'mon, tell me," she said, while she looked up into his deep brown eyes. She knew he was cute, and that her girlfriends watching from the sidelines must be envying her.

"Okay," Nick said, "but will you promise you won't laugh?"

"I won't. I promise," she said.

"I go to Oklahoma State," he said, and this time, his grin broke into a laugh.

"Are you serious?" Sara said. "I'm going there in the fall."

Nick's attempt at a joke backfired. He was going into his sophomore year, and Sara was a summer away from starting her freshman year at the same school. Oklahoma was anything but a small school, and most of her graduating class wanted to go there.

Nick had picked Sara out from a group of girls standing alongside the dance floor. He was especially drawn to her light blonde hair and red parka. It lit up her features, her twinkling eyes, and welcoming smile.

"Isn't that amazing?" she said. "Who would've thought we'd be going to the same school, since we didn't go to the same high school, and we live on opposite sides of the city? What a coincidence!"

That night, a relationship began between Sara and Nick that was to blossom into marriage four years later. Everyone assumed they would marry at the end of their college days. There had never been anyone else for either of them, and they knew they were to marry each other. That's all they knew. Neither had been raised in a family that modeled healthy relationships, but Sara and Nick didn't know how that fact would affect them.

One plus One Equals?

Nick entered the business world and Sara that of teaching upon graduation. They had been taught to work hard by hard working parents. Nothing had ever been given to them unless they worked for it, and they approached their new jobs and their marriage with that attitude.

Sara plunged into her teaching assignment vigorously, staying up late doing lesson plans and grading papers. Nick's new job took him out of town and away from home for multiple nights at a time.

"What city are you going to this time?" Sara asked Nick as she combed her hair and blew the smoke from her cigarette.

"Kansas City," he said. "I wish I didn't have to go. I feel like I just got home."

"You did," Sara said. "I'm not sure I would've married you if you had told me you would be traveling all the time."

"It's not *all* the time," said Nick.

"It feels like *all* the time. It's impossible to plan anything, because you're never here."

"There's nothing I can do about it. It's my job. I can't quit. We've already got so many things we have to pay for, and your salary is not enough."

"That's fine. I'll have to learn to be on my own without you then." Her tone was sharp and condemning as anger spilled from her lips.

She turned on her heel and walked away. She didn't kiss him goodbye, and as she grabbed the keys to the car with the huge loan balance on it, she knew Nick was right about the amount of money they owed. They'd bought so many things to furnish their apartment, and the thought of two jobs and two salaries gave them confidence that they could afford just about anything. They were a couple with payment plans and credit cards.

"Just because we owe money on our credit cards doesn't excuse his traveling and the nights I spend alone," she muttered to herself as she started the car.

"I have to go to Washington State for a month," said Nick one cold Monday morning. "They want me to go through some sales training. It could mean a promotion and more money."

Sara looked up from her coffee. "But you already spend so much time away from home. A whole month? What am I supposed to do here for a month?"

"It'll go fast, you'll see. A month isn't really that long a time. Just think, if I were in the army, I'd be gone for months, maybe even a year."

"But you're not in the military, and we've just gotten married. I feel like I don't know you anymore, because I hardly ever see you. Going away for a month just makes it worse. Won't you be able to come home during that month, and when will you leave?" Hot anger rose up in her throat, and she burned with indignation.

"I'll find out the specifics today, and I'll let you know tonight."

"I might not be home tonight," she said, deciding that she could play the game, too, of not being home at night.

Nick looked quizzically, confused by her response. *What can I do?* he thought. *I can't quit my job. I signed a contract that I would work for them for at least three years. She's being unreasonable.*

The Unwelcome News

That month apart from Nick marked a revelation for Sara. "I'm pregnant!" she told Nick during a telephone conversation. "It couldn't come at a worse time. You're gone, and now you're telling me that we'll be moving! I don't think I can take any more bad news."

"It'll all work out," said Nick. "We always said we wanted to have kids, even though it's coming earlier than we planned. I'm still excited."

"Well, I'm not. I'll have to quit my job here and move to a new place. What will I do about a job and all our bills? I won't have any help with a baby in a strange town with no friends."

Sara's disappointment in Nick and her marriage had mushroomed with every day that Nick was gone, and now, a baby? This was the icing on the cake—a very ruined cake.

"Did you want to get pregnant?" said Sara's teaching partner, Beth, a woman whose decision had been to place her career before a family. She didn't like children and couldn't understand those who did. Sara understood her views and felt uncomfortable telling Beth of her pregnancy. Beth was very judgmental of anyone who would give up her teaching position to have children.

"No, but now that it's here, there's nothing I can do," said Sara.

"Yes, there is," said Beth. "How about an abortion? It certainly would solve the problem."

"Oh, I couldn't," said Sara. "That would be a sin."

Beth chuckled. "You're kidding, aren't you? Where in the world did you get that idea?"

Sara had been raised a Roman Catholic, although she hadn't been in a church since their wedding day.

"I believe it would be wrong to have an abortion. I might not go to church, but I just think that it's wrong."

"Suit yourself," said Beth, "but you know what a pregnancy means for your job, don't you? And now, you're moving out of state, too? That sure does complicate everything, doesn't it?"

"Everything that could go wrong is going wrong," said Sara. "I feel like I'm slipping into a black hole, and I can't get out. If one more bad thing happens to me, I don't think I can handle it."

R-r-r-ring. The doorbell rang for what seemed like an eternity until Jackie, Sara's neighbor, peered through the screen door.

"Sara, what's wrong? You look like you've seen a ghost," Jackie said as she opened the door wide. Have you just come home from school?"

"I just got home, and I've noticed some spotting, some bleeding, and I'm a little scared. I don't know what to do. I knew you'd know what's happening."

"First, let's call your doctor. Give me his number, and I'll dial it for you," said Jackie in a consoling tone.

After talking to the office, Jackie handed the phone to Sara. "It's your doctor."

"Yes, Dr. Callaway, I'll go to bed and rest. When can you see me?"

Sara couldn't see her doctor for days, so she went back to work the next day. She didn't like shirking her teaching duties, and she wasn't really sure what was happening with the pregnancy.

"I am in a lot of pain," Sara told Beth as she entered the teachers' lounge.

"Do you want me to call someone?" Beth responded.

She looked at Sara's face and immediately knew she was suffering and in trouble. "I'm calling 911," she said.

After what seemed like an eternity, two paramedics were wheeling a stretcher down the school hallway, and they stopped outside the teachers' lounge.

Sara doubled over on the sofa, and the medics lifted her onto the stretcher. Overhead, the fluorescent lights illuminated her plight, and students and teachers ogled the stretcher as it passed between them.

The Loss

"Don't touch me," said Sara, as Nick leaned over her hospital bed to kiss her cheek. "This wouldn't have happened if you were here."

Nick didn't answer. He knew Sara was groggy from the anesthesia, but how was this miscarriage his fault?

He was in Seattle when he got the call that Sara was in the hospital. Catching the first flight home, he rushed to her room. Surprised at her accusation, he hoped it was based upon shock or stress.

"How are you feeling, honey?" said Nick as he took her hand.

Sara turned her face away from him and stared out the window. It was an overcast, rainy day, and the atmosphere in the hospital room was just as gray. She and Nick had not discussed the pregnancy and the baby, and now the doors slammed shut on any discussion.

"I'm sorry I wasn't here for you when all this happened, but I got here as quickly as I could. I'm so glad there was someone at school to help you, and that the paramedics took good care of you.

I know you're sad you lost the baby, and I'm sad, too. We're in this together, honey. I'm going to see if I can postpone the move."

Sara's reaction wasn't sadness. "I'm so angry I could scream," she said. "Leave me alone. I don't want to talk to you, to anyone."

Sara was released from the hospital, and she and Nick never spoke of the miscarriage. By the end of the month, they were living in a new city, knowing no one. Nick's job carried more responsibility and necessitated more travel. With the promotion came more time away from home. He and Sara lived in their home together, but they were seldom together. The recipe was brewing for an impending disaster.

4

Migraine Headaches

Nick opened the front door with trepidation. He had news for Sara, but he knew it was something she would not want to hear.

"Hi, honey, are you home?" he said in the cheeriest voice he could muster. He walked past the living room and saw the twins, Michael and Madison, their eyes glued to the television.

"Hi, guys," he said, but he received no acknowledgment.

Moving toward the rear bedrooms, he saw the drapes drawn in their bedroom. Sara lay on their bed, her eyes covered with a washcloth and an ice bag.

"Another headache?" he said softly, knowing that Sara could not tolerate loud noises or voices when she had one of her headaches.

She didn't answer him. She thought, *What's wrong with you? Can't you see I have a headache? Are you that stupid?* But she said nothing to her husband.

"I have some news for you, but we'll talk later. Maybe I'll take the twins out for dinner. That would make it an easier night. I can get you something if you'd like."

He knew she usually didn't eat when she had a migraine, because it caused her an upset stomach. He asked and offered anyway. Still, there was no answer from the woman lying in the darkness. Their marriage had deteriorated more and more each year, until they barely talked.

"C'mon, kids, let's go out and get some pizza. How does that sound?" He picked up the remote, turned off the television, and stood between them and the television. He finally had their attention.

"Dad, we were watching that," said Michael, groaning at his father.

"Let's go," said Nick. "Your mom isn't feeling well. I thought we'd get out of the house for a while and let her rest. Besides, I need to talk to you about something important."

Michael and Madison were fraternal twins who had changed schools every two years of their school lives. They had heard the line, "We need to talk," too many times, and both sensed something was coming. They looked at each other and at their father warily.

"Oh, no, here we go again," said Michael.

Michael and Madison were each other's best friend, but they had great difficulty making new friends. Each time either developed a close friendship, he or she was uprooted and moved to another city and another school. They were tired of starting over.

Sitting at the Pizza Palace, the twins eagerly reached for their slices of pizza. Nick tried to make small talk, but they weren't interested.

"So, where are we moving this time?" Madison said. She knew her father all too well and recognized his "We need to talk" line.

"Connecticut," said Nick. "It's a good job, and I think you both will really like the town."

"Seriously? We just got settled here. Have you told Mom yet?" Michael said.

"No," he said. "I didn't want to upset her while she's not feeling well."

"You know there won't be any good time to tell her. She's going to be upset."

Nick turned and saw a tear trickling down Madison's cheek. "I just made the girls' basketball team today. I haven't even had a chance to tell Mom, and now that's over, too."

Nick tried to talk to his children about the move, but they just looked down at their pizza. Having lost his appetite, Michael said, "Dad, I think we need to go home."

Morning

The family sat at the breakfast table, staring somberly and saying nothing. Sara shuffled to the table, her hair disheveled and her worn, stained bathrobe thrown over her nightgown.

"What's wrong?" she said to her children. "What's going on? Why are you both so sad this morning?"

Neither spoke, but both looked at their father.

"Go ahead, Dad, tell her. Why don't you ruin her day, too?" said Michael.

Nick gulped and said, "I'm being transferred to Connecticut. The manager there quit, and they want me to take his—"

"You've got to be kidding!" said Sara. "We haven't unpacked all the boxes in the garage yet. I don't care who quit his job. Why does it have to be you who takes his place?"

"If I want to be considered for promotions, I have to take this position. It will all work out, I promise you. The kids will be all right. They're resilient. They always adapt."

Michelle and Michael got up from their seats and left the table in unison.

"He has no clue," muttered Madison as she grabbed her backpack. "He just has no clue," she said, shaking her head from side to side.

Nick and Sara sat staring at each other, and Nick was afraid of what was coming next. In past arguments when Sara got angry and screamed, he couldn't say anything to make things better. She quickly would get past the point of being able to listen.

Sara pushed her dish and coffee cup toward Nick. "I've had it. I can't take any more in this marriage. This isn't a marriage. The kids and I have followed you all over this country, and for what? Your job? How about for us? Have you ever thought about how hard this is for us? We have no friends, because we never stay in one place long enough to make any. Your kids are drowning, and you don't see it. They stay to themselves all the time. Thank God, they have each other. We're dying in this house, and all you can think about is your job and your promotions. Well, good luck with that!"

Sara walked toward the sink and began throwing dishes into it with abandon. She banged dishes against each other and slammed cupboard doors, their noise drowning out Nick's next words.

"I need to give my boss an answer," he said, as he picked up his briefcase and opened the kitchen door.

Sara's rage broke into tears, and she walked haltingly to the den sofa. She sank into the soft cushions, and gloom descended upon her like a shroud.

"Oh, no, not again," Sara muttered, covering her eyes with her hands. Pain stung her temple and traveled above her eyes. Within minutes, her head was held in a viselike grip of another migraine headache. Nausea overtook her stomach as she felt the room spinning. She knew the drill, and soon she would be on the bathroom floor with her head over the toilet.

"How can I make these headaches stop?" she said. "I hate my life. I hate it."

You're Looking for Jesus

Rrrrrrring. Sara opened the front door. Boxes were piled high in the living room behind her.

"Hi, I'm Emma from next door. I brought you a pot of soup. I figured you could use it for your family. I bet you haven't found the boxes with your kitchen stuff yet."

"Oh, everything is such a mess," said Sara. "The movers finished unloading everything late last night. I'm Sara."

She took the soup tureen from Emma. "I'd ask you in, but you can hardly find a path to walk."

"That's okay, I wanted to welcome you to the neighborhood. We all try to help each other here. I'd be happy to help you unpack if you would like."

"No, thanks, but I appreciate the offer."

"Please let me know if I can help you. We're not a big town, but you might want to know where to shop, the best place to get your hair done—stuff like that. Connecticut is a great state, and here everyone knows his neighbor. I'm happy to help you. Some people in this neighborhood did that for Jim and me when we moved here, and I'd like to do the same for you, if you'll let me."

"Thanks, I'll let you know."

Emma had taped a calling card to the tureen. It contained her name, address, phone number, and picture. She was serious about her offer.

Sara closed the door and walked into the kitchen, setting the soup on the counter in the only empty space she could find.

Wow, what a friendly lady. I don't think I've ever met anyone so nice. To think, she actually offered to help me unpack. Maybe I should've let her. I don't even know where to start. She sat on a stack of boxes and looked at the daunting task.

Nick had left early for his new job, and the twins didn't want to miss any more school, so the house was empty. Just Sara and the boxes.

Rethinking Emma's offer, Sara walked next door and rang her new neighbor's doorbell.

"I'm sorry I was so short with you," said Sara. "I've never experienced anyone offering to help me unpack in all our moves,

44

so you caught me off guard. I'd love some help, if you're still game."

"Let me get some drinks and snacks for us, and we'll make short work of that kitchen," she said. "We've moved a lot, too, so I'm used to unpacking boxes. How about if I unpack and you put away?"

"That would be great," said Sara as they entered her foyer. There was something different about this new neighbor, but she couldn't put her finger on it. She just knew she was different.

Months later, as Nick, Sara, and the twins settled into their new home, Emma appeared at Sara's door with a plate of chocolate chip cookies, Nick's favorite.

"I made some extra, and I thought your family might enjoy these. I love to bake, and I also love to share."

Sara never met anyone as nice as Emma. At first, she didn't know how to react, but she decided that she was a genuinely nice person, the first neighbor her family had met in Connecticut.

"Emma," said Sara as they enjoyed some coffee with the cookies, "I would like to find a church where we can take the twins. Do you know of a good one?"

Emma responded with a strange statement. She knew she had Sara's trust, so she told her what she believed with all her heart.

"Sara, you're not looking for a church. You're looking for Jesus."

Sara didn't understand what she meant, because she didn't think she was looking for Jesus.

How can I look for Jesus? she thought. *And, where can I find him?*

Her neighbor's saying rolled around in her mind for hours and days, and she still did not understand its meaning.

The Ornament

Christmas was fast approaching, and one morning Emma appeared on Sara's doorstep with a Bible and a small package tied with a red bow.

"May I come in?" she said.

"Of course," said Sara. "I was just thinking about what a difference having you as a neighbor has made for me with this move."

"I appreciate that," said Emma. "Here, I brought you something." She stretched out her hand and put the small package in Sara's hands.

Inside the box was an ornament of the nativity scene—a stable with Mary, Joseph, and the infant Jesus. Sara looked at it and didn't know what to say.

"I know you're looking for Jesus, and I thought I could help you find him," said Emma.

"We've been going to church," said Sara, "but we haven't heard much about Jesus. I think I'm a Christian. I mean, I'm going to church now."

"Going to church doesn't make a person a Christian. It's what you believe about Jesus Christ that matters. What do you believe about Jesus Christ?"

"I believe he is God," said Sara. "That's about all I know. I had a crucifix over my bed as a kid."

Emma had a Bible in her hand. Sara had never known anyone who read the Bible, and she didn't have one.

"Would you mind if I showed you what the Bible says about Jesus Christ?"

"Okay," said Sara. The two women walked into the den and sat down on the overstuffed couch. Emma opened her Bible to the first chapter of the Book of John.

"In the beginning was the Word, and the Word was with God, and the Word was God. He was in the beginning with God. All things were made through him, and without him was not any thing made that was made. In him was life, and the life was the light of men. The light shines in the darkness, and the darkness has not overcome it."

"He was in the world, and the world was made through him, yet the world did not know him. He came to his own, and his own people did not receive him. But to all who did receive him, who believed in his name, he gave the right to become children of God, who were born, not of blood nor of the will of the flesh nor of the will of man, but of God" (John 1:1–5; 10–13, English Standard Version).

"The Word is Jesus Christ, and what do we learn about the Word, Jesus, from these verses?" said Emma.

"He's God, he's always existed, and the Word gave life and light to everyone."

"That's great," said Emma, "but do you see in verse eleven that his own people rejected him?"

"Yes," said Sara.

"But, in verse twelve, it tells us that all who believed him and accepted him became God's children with a birth that comes from God. Let me read you some more verses. Are you tracking with me?"

"I'm with you," said Sara.

She turned more pages and landed upon the third chapter of the Book of Romans, verses 22–25. "How about if you read these verses this time?"

"Sure," said Sara, as she began, "'the righteousness of God through faith in Jesus Christ for all who believe. For there is no distinction, for all have sinned and fall short of the glory of God, and are justified by his grace as a gift, through the redemption that is in Christ Jesus, whom God put forward as a propitiation by his blood, to be received by faith.'"

"So, if I believe in Jesus, I can be forgiven for my sins?" said Sara.

"You must believe that Jesus Christ shed his blood on the cross as a penalty for your sin, to pay for your sins before a just and a holy God, and that there is nothing you can do to earn forgiveness. Placing your faith in Jesus as the one who died for you, paid the penalty for you, and forgives you of all your sins—past, present, and future—is what saves you from that penalty, makes you right with Father God, and gives you salvation. Jesus is the key to salvation, forgiveness, and life itself. He came into the world to give his life and light to all who would believe in him. Are you ready to believe in him and accept him into your life because of what he has done for you?"

"Yes, I am," said Sara. "I want to accept Jesus Christ into my life and believe in him. I have done so many wrong things in my life. I need his forgiveness."

"That's why he came to this earth, and that's why we celebrate Christmas. It was his destiny to come and die so that we could live."

Sara and Emma joined hands. "Sara, would you like me to pray, and would you like to repeat the prayer after me?"

Sara had never prayed, so Emma's offer took her anxiety away.

"Yes," she said.

Emma prayed, and Sara repeated every word.

"Dear Lord Jesus, I believe that you are God, that you have always existed, and that you came to earth to die on the cross to save me and forgive me of my sins. I ask you to forgive me today for all my sins, for all the horrible things I've done, all my anger towards everyone. I believe that if I accept you and believe in you, I can be forgiven. I ask you to come into my life as my Savior, my Lord, and my very life. I believe that you came to give me your life and your light. Please give me your life, Lord, and I will love you for all of my days. Amen."

Sara opened her eyes, looked up, and felt a wash of peace flood her body.

"I feel like a very heavy weight just left me and was taken off my shoulders. What was that?"

"Do you remember when I told you that you were looking for Jesus? Well, you just found him, or, more importantly, he's found you."

5

The Breakfast Meeting

Nick slid into the booth at the IHOP restaurant. "Hey, how are you this morning?" he said to his friend, Steve.

Steve was a salesman under Nick's management in the small Connecticut town, and they met regularly at IHOP to discuss business. This morning, Steve was especially anxious to talk to Nick.

"I'm doing great," said Steve. "I have some news to tell you."

"What is it?" said Nick.

Nick was always impressed by Steve's attitude. He was a good salesman, and his attitude was positive and upbeat.

"I've decided to go to seminary. I want to become a pastor of a church."

"I don't understand," said Nick. "Are you quitting your job?"

"Yes, Sofia and I decided this was the best time in our lives to make this change. Our kids are all in school, and Sofia can work while I go to seminary. She's willing to support me."

"I've never known anyone who quit his job to go to seminary," said Nick. "I've known priests, but I don't know anything about becoming a pastor."

"I don't either, yet. I know that's what I want to do. I want to teach people about Jesus Christ and how much he loves them."

Nick lowered his head. "C'mon, Steve, aren't you taking this religion stuff a little too far?"

"Nick," said Steve. "Let's say you walked out of here this morning, got into your car, and got onto I-95. You're driving along, and out of nowhere, an eighteen-wheeler broadsided you. In a split second, you stood in front of St. Peter at the pearly gates of heaven, and he said to you, 'Nick, what right do you have to come into my heaven?' What would you say to him, Nick?"

"Well, I guess I'd say that I'd been a good person, never killed anyone, and tried to treat people the way I wanted them to treat me."

"What if the person coming after you had been a better person and had treated people better than you had? Where's the cut-off point? Who decides how good you would have to be to get into heaven?"

"I don't know. God, I guess."

"Yes, God does. But the thing is, no one can do enough good things or be good enough. God is holy and perfect, and he requires us to be perfect and without sin to enter heaven. Do you qualify?"

"No," said Nick.

"That's why Jesus Christ came to this earth. He knew we could never be good enough, and that we would all sin and fall short of what God would require."

"But I haven't been that bad," said Nick.

"Sin is missing the mark. Have you ever missed the mark, in your marriage, your job, anything, Nick?"

"I'm sure I have, lots of times."

"Well, missing it once is as bad as missing it a million times. Sin is sin, and sin has no place in heaven. That's why we needed Jesus to come and die on the cross for our sins, so we could be forgiven. When he died, he paid for every one of your sins, and mine, so you could have a pathway to God the Father through his death, burial, and resurrection."

"You know, Steve, I've never heard anything like this before. How do you know all this?"

"Because I'm a Christian, and I know what the Bible says. It is full of truth about God and Jesus. They are God, and Jesus Christ died for you so you could receive his forgiveness and accept his life into your heart. Do you believe he died for you, Nick?"

"Yes, I do," he said.

"Then today, you can receive his salvation into your life. Tell him you believe in him and his death on the cross for you to save you from your sins. If you do, he will forgive you and come into your life."

Nick sat mesmerized, unable to move. He smiled at Steve and took it all in. Eventually, he arose, shook Steve's hand, walked out of the restaurant, and got into his car. He knew that day that if anything happened to him, he was going to heaven. As he put his car in drive, he prayed a prayer, the first one of his life.

"Jesus, thank you for dying for me to forgive me for my sins. I know I could never be good enough to deserve heaven, and that you gave your life for me to be forgiven. Would you please make us a Christian family?" He drove along the highway while cleansing tears streamed down his face. A sense of peace filled the car, and Nick had never felt a presence with him, but this morning, he felt someone was in the car with him.

The Homecoming

Nick walked into his home, and Sara greeted him as she came out of the kitchen. The smells wafting from the kitchen filled his nostrils. It had been a long time since Sara had cooked dinner. By this time of the day, she was usually in bed with a migraine.

"What kind of a day have you had?" she said.

"A very unusual one," he said. "I met with one of my salesmen, Steve, and he quit his job to enter the seminary. He said he wants to become a pastor. I don't understand that, but I respect his decision. He's a really nice guy, and I like him a lot. We had a very interesting conversation."

"About what?" said Sara.

"About God. I learned some things that I didn't know, and I'm still rolling them around in my mind."

Sara took Nick's hand and told him of her encounter with her neighbor Emma.

A New Journey, but Old Problems

"Emma, can the twins and I go to church with you? Nick left this morning on one of his trips, and I'd like to visit your church."

"Absolutely," said Emma. "We'll swing by and pick you and the kids up around ten."

"Aw, Mom, do we have to?" said Michael when he learned of Sara's decision to take him to church. "I need to work on a project, and I have a soccer game this afternoon."

"Yes," she said. "I want us to go to church as a family."

"But what about Dad? Why doesn't he have to go, too?"

"He will. He's just not home today. He's already on his way to the airport. Come on, Mike, this is important to me. We've left God out of our lives, and we need to change that."

Mike dragged himself out of bed, walked into the bathroom, and turned on the shower while Sara entered Madison's room armed with the same directive.

Sara, Michael, and Madison got involved in church activities while Nick continued to travel, necessitating his absence from both church and family activities. Sara and Nick were Christians now, but their circumstances remained the same.

"Nick, I want to take a class at church called Christianity 101. Can you take it with me?"

"When does it meet?" he said.

"Wednesday nights, before the church service."

"You know that's the worst night of the week for me. I can't plan for something on that night, because I could be out of town."

"Nothing's changed," said Sara. "I can't count on you to be here for anything. I'm getting so tired of being alone and handling the twins, their activities, and now church on my own. We never see you, and when we do, you're getting ready for your next trip."

"I know," said Nick. "I'm sorry that my job takes me away, but I have no control over that. It's my job. I realize I'm missing a lot at home, but can you just hang in there a while longer? Maybe something will change."

"You say that all the time, and nothing changes. Our kids will be gone from home in a few years, and you have missed their growing up years because you put your job first."

"I can never do anything right in this family," he said. "In your eyes, I'm always a loser, failing at being a husband and a father. The only success I have is with my job. I'm appreciated there, even if I'm not at home."

"I'm not calling you a failure," she said. "I just want you home more. It's a lonely life raising kids on your own, and I've done it for years. We're Christians, and our family should come first."

Nick felt that he was caught between a rock and a hard place with nowhere to turn. "God, please help me," he prayed. "I can't make Sara happy, or anyone, for that matter."

Nick arranged his schedule so he could be home on Wednesday evenings to take the class with Sara. She was happy for a time, but, when the class ended, Nick's travel schedule resumed.

"I'm tired of arguing about my job," said Nick one Monday morning. "Maybe you should've married someone else, someone who worked out of his home and could be here all the time."

"Crash!" The coffee cup broke into jagged pieces as it was hurled against the side of the sink.

"That's not what I want," said Sara. "You exaggerate what I said. I want you to have a normal job, like everyone else."

"I need to go. We argue about this all the time, and there is never a solution. I don't know why you get so angry. That's the third cup you've broken. I wish you'd settle down."

Sara grabbed her head as she watched Nick get into his car and slam the door. Pain stabbed her in the eye, and she knew she'd soon be in bed with a migraine headache. They had lessened for a while, right after she became a Christian, but this one was back with a vengeance.

"What can I do?" moaned Sara as she rolled her head onto her pillow? "I'm so unhappy. We're both Christians, but I can't make our marriage work. I feel like I'm losing control—of everything."

The next morning, Nick appeared in the kitchen with his packed suitcase and announced that he was leaving. Emma called later that day with the name of the counselor who had helped her and Jim. Sara was desperate and was willing to try anything, even counseling.

6

The Counseling Process

"I've hit a wall, and nothing I've tried to do in our marriage to make things better has worked," said Sara to Dr. Campbell.

"First," he said, "I want you to realize you're here for yourself and not to change your husband. Only God can do that. It is beyond your capability and not in your control."

"I know that. The Lord knows I've tried to change Nick. He's just so stubborn and won't listen to me."

"Sara, are you willing to let God work in your life, to transform the way you think and respond, and use your circumstances to do something new in you?"

"I think so, although that sounds kind of scary to me. I've been this way my whole life. What will that look like, that something new?"

Dr. Campbell said, "We've all been programmed since birth to think and act a certain way in response either to acceptance or rejection in our lives. When you become a Christian, you walk into this new life in Christ with patterns that are not honoring or glorifying to Jesus Christ. I'd like to take your history, to learn about how you got to where you are. I have a sentence that I tell my clients. 'Jesus gave his life for you so he could give his life to you, so he could live his life through you.' Where do you fit in that sentence?"

"I guess I am in the beginning. I believe that Jesus gave his life for me."

"Have you accepted Jesus Christ into your life as your Savior?"

"Yes, I have," said Sara.

"Then Jesus gave you his life the moment you accepted him, through the person of his Holy Spirit. Jesus gave his life *to* you."

"Okay," said Sara. "I believe that."

"The reason you are here is that you don't understand how to let Jesus live his life through you. Do you agree with me?"

"I do," she said.

"Then, let's begin by talking about your life, your childhood, your growing up years, up until today. I want to know you and where you have been. Are you ready to begin?"

"Yes," she said sheepishly.

"Tell me about the first five years of your life. What can you tell me about your mother and your father? Help me to get to know them."

"Well, my father had his own business and ran it out of our house. My mother helped him by answering the phone and taking care of the customers when they called. I didn't see him much. He was seldom home, and I don't remember much else about him. My mother pretty much was at his beck and call, because he was so busy with his business and needed her help with the phone. She cooked his breakfast early in the morning, before anyone was up, and stayed up until almost midnight keeping his dinner warm. He came home after I was in bed, so I didn't see him most days."

"Tell me, Sara, do you remember anything especially traumatic or fearful happening to you in those early years, say from age five through elementary school?"

Dr. Campbell looked at Sara's face. "What's wrong?" he said. "You look scared. Your face is pale, almost ashen."

Sara looked down at her hands and swallowed hard. Her mouth was dry, and there was no saliva to help with her swallow. She coughed and choked as she tried not to answer.

"I've never talked about this with anyone."

"Can you tell me what happened?" said Dr. Campbell.

"There was this boy, one of my brother's friends. He lived in the house behind us. He used to put me up on his shoulders and carry me around."

"How did that make you feel?" he said.

"It made me feel special, like he really liked me. No one had ever played with me like that before."

"What did he do?"

"He carried me on his shoulders and played with us kids. We played hide-and-go-seek out in his backyard. After a while, he carried me down into his basement. There were big doors that opened up into the yard, and we went down the steps."

"Tell me what you remember about that time."

"The stairs were concrete, and the cellar was cold and damp. There were a lot of old furniture pieces there, and it looked like no one ever cleaned it. It made me scared, but he told me not to be afraid, that he would take care of me."

"What else did he tell you?"

"He told me we were going to play doctor, and he was going to operate on me. He was the doctor and I was the patient."

"What else do you remember?"

Tears trickled down Sara's face, and she clutched her chest. Her breathing labored heavily, and she gasped for air.

"You're having a panic attack," said Dr. Campbell.

He took her hands and prayed, "Dear Lord, please calm Sara and take away the panic she feels when she thinks of this event. Help her to breathe, Lord."

Sara opened her eyes and looked with worry at the doctor. Her breathing normalized, but she didn't continue.

"I really don't want to talk about this," she said.

"We're going to have to, eventually," he said. "It obviously causes you a great deal of anxiety and pain, and I believe that's been stuffed way down inside your heart for a long time, since you were a little girl."

"Can we talk about it another time?" she said. "My head is starting to hurt."

Dr. Campbell said, "Do you think we can talk about your family for a little while, until the end of our session?"

"I suppose."

"How many siblings did you have, and what were your relationships like with them?"

"I had two brothers and a sister, all much older than I. My sister was thirteen years older than I, the next brother eight years older, and the next brother four years older. I don't remember having a relationship with any of them. I was the youngest, and none of them paid attention to me."

"Who did pay attention to you?"

"I guess my mom must have, although I don't remember much. I'm sure my dad didn't, because he was never home— worked all the time with his business. He paid attention to my brothers, because they worked for him when they became teenagers. My sister did, too. Our family was all about dad's work. I was the baby of the family, and I couldn't help in the business, so I got left out. I honestly don't remember anyone ever taking care of me. I'm sure there was someone. I just don't remember. It has always bothered me that I don't have any good memories of my childhood, not until I was in school. There must've been some good. I hope so. I just don't remember anything really good. That makes me sad."

"Tell me what you remember about your school years."

"I was a very good student—straight As. I loved school, because I was pretty smart and loved my teachers."

"Why did you love your teachers?"

"Because they paid attention to me and let me do special things."

"Was there any teacher who particularly stands out?"

"Yes, she was my English teacher. She let me correct the papers for the class."

"How did that make you feel?"

"Special. Important. I guess that's why I loved school so much. I had a place there, a purpose."

"And how did you feel when you went home?"

"Lost. Alone. Pretty worthless. That's terrible, isn't it?"

"Those are the feelings you had inside you, and they shaped you and what you believed about yourself in a lot of ways. So, where do you suppose you got your value, your worth?"

"I guess from school, from doing well, and from being well-liked by my teachers."

"Did you have many friends?" said Dr. Campbell.

"Yes, because I was smart I was friends with the kids who did well, and we were favored by everyone—the teachers, principals, etc. School was my world. I was happy there."

"We must close this session for today. I want you to do some reading and listening this coming week. I have a book for you to read, some verses in the Bible, and some messages to hear. Can you do that for me?"

"I'll try," said Sara. "Do you think this will help my marriage?"

"I believe it will help you, which will have an effect upon your relationships. I can't promise that it will save your marriage, but often, as a life changes, others are affected in a positive way. We just have to see what the Lord does through this. I want you to do your homework, be on time for your appointments, and trust God with this process. Don't try to be in control of everything. He wants to carry you through this. I know that sounds hard to do, but today was the first step. Let's pray and ask God to enable you to talk about the neighbor boy next week, okay?"

Dr. Campbell closed the session asking God to prepare Sara for their next session together. Sara left the office both hopeful for change and anxious about the next appointment.

The Neighbor

It took several weeks until Sara trusted Dr. Campbell enough to divulge the details about the neighbor boy. During one session, she felt peace as she opened her mouth to tell her counselor about the abuse. All of a sudden, words came tumbling out, cascading like a waterfall in a torrent of tears.

"He hurt me," she said, "and, when I look back on it, I have no idea why I let him take me into that basement."

"How old were you?" said Dr. Campbell.

"Six years old."

"A six-year-old child trusts everyone and is so innocent," he said. "You had no idea that he had any ill intentions."

"I thought he was like a big brother. He was Alan's big brother, and I thought he was like my family, because Alan and I were best friends. I didn't understand what was happening until it was too late."

"Had your mother ever warned you about letting someone touch you inappropriately?"

"No. I don't think my parents knew anything about sexual abuse back then. My parents never really instructed me about that or staying away from strangers. I had free reign and went wherever I wanted and played with the neighborhood children. I guess they trusted everyone. I'm sure I did."

"And this boy told you to trust him, too," said her counselor.

"I did. That was a mistake."

"Can you tell me what he did to you?"

"I don't want to go into detail. He kept telling me he was operating on me, and he put his hands where he shouldn't have. When I think about it, I believe I was numb. I didn't understand.

I was so little. I must've been terribly stupid to let him touch me and hurt me."

"You were six, and an innocent little girl. A six-year-old who knew nothing of not allowing someone to touch you inappropriately, who had never been taught how to be wary of a boy like your neighbor. It wasn't your fault. He was the perpetrator, and he obviously thought he could get away with it. How long did it go on, and how did it come to an end?"

"I don't know. It's all such a blur. I must've told someone, and I don't remember that. All I remember is one day his parents and he were in our living room with my parents and me."

"Do you realize that he committed a crime? Did he receive any type punishment, or did your parents report him to the police?"

"No, not to my knowledge. I sat in our living room, and no one spoke to me. My parents and his talked, and they got up and left. The next thing I knew I was punished and not allowed to play with his little brother anymore or go into his yard. It was like it was all my fault."

"When you think of that boy, how do you feel?"

"Scared. I have a nightmare about him every night that he's chasing me. Then I feel guilty when I see him coming towards me. I run away to escape."

"Why do you feel guilty? Real guilt comes from real sin. Did you commit a sin according to the Word of God?"

"I don't know. I shouldn't have let him touch me. I should've stopped him."

"Could you have stopped him or left the basement?"

"No. He held me down on the glider with his hands and put my legs under him. I guess I was like a captured bird in a snare. I couldn't get out."

"So, where is your sin? He's the one who not only sinned against you, but he committed a crime for which he should've been reported to the police. Your parents didn't do that. I don't know why. Perhaps they were shocked and didn't know to report it."

"When I look back on it now, I suppose I was the victim. The whole thing has always made me feel so guilty and dirty, like there's something wrong with me. Why did he pick me? Was there something wrong with me? Did I give off some kind of vibe that he could molest me?"

"No, certainly not. You were six years old. He knew you were alone, and your family wasn't around to protect you. You said you were on your own in the neighborhood, and I'm sure he knew that. People who sexually abuse children look for the loners, those who have no one watching out for them. He knew your family, that you were the youngest, and that you were alone. It was an opportunity for him to take advantage of you."

"So it wasn't my fault?"

"No, Sara, it wasn't your fault. When you think about this boy, what kind of feelings surface?"

"Besides fear—anger. Lots of anger. I never realized I was so angry about it. But I am very angry. Nick tells me often that I am an angry person, but I never thought I was. I can feel it inside now."

"Do you believe that you could forgive him for what he did to you?"

"No, I can't forgive him. I think he ruined my life. I have dreamed about him since I was six years old, up until this day. I'm sure it has affected other things, too, that I haven't been aware of."

Brokenness

During one of Sara's counseling sessions, Dr. Campbell talked of brokenness and surrender of everything in her life to Jesus Christ. He said that perhaps Nick's leaving home was God's way of breaking her of her doing everything in her own strength.

"Ever since you've been a little girl, you performed for others' acceptance, and school and your studies were a prime example. That just hasn't been working in your marriage with Nick. He's left, and that is the ultimate rejection for a spouse."

"That's true," she said. "I feel like I never did enough, like whatever I did wasn't good enough for him. That's funny, now that I say it aloud. Nick has said exactly the same thing to me. I guess we make each other feel like we can't measure up. That's pretty weird, isn't it?"

"No, not really. Sometimes the faults we see in others are the very ones we do ourselves. It's always easier to point out other people's faults than to look at our own. Do you know what God wants you to do with all that performing for acceptance?"

"No," she said.

"He wants you to give up. You don't have to perform for his acceptance. He has already accepted you because Jesus died for you. You are accepted by God because he accepts Jesus totally. Let me show you how God placed you into Christ when He saved you. Thus, his acceptance becomes yours. You are accepted because you are in Christ. You can give up performing for him and everyone else. You are already accepted, not because of your performance but because you're in Christ. Because of the sexual abuse you endured as a child, you spent the rest of your life trying to be good enough and not feel guilty. You did that by working hard for other people's acceptance. God is bringing all that to an end. It is part of the breaking process he's taking you through."

"Does that mean that God doesn't want me to work for him? I've always heard that we need to *do things for God* because he saved us. I thought I was saved to serve him."

"God saved you through Jesus Christ so he could live his life in and through you, and through that receive glory. The Christian life is all about what he does through you for his glory, not about what *you* do *for him* in your own strength. You don't have to work for him in order for him to love and accept you. You are already loved and accepted. Just accept that as truth. Let me show you a verse from the Bible. 'To the praise of the glory of his grace, by which he made us accepted in the Beloved' (Eph. 1:6, NKJV)."

"Wow, that's huge for me. I feel like I've been working so hard for acceptance all my life, and since I became a Christian, I've been trying hard to earn God's acceptance. I've never felt like I've made it."

"You can give that up today and receive his acceptance of you just as you are without working for it. How would that make you feel?"

"Relieved, I think."

"Let's pray," said Dr. Campbell. "Just repeat these words in your heart as I pray them. Dear Jesus, today I give up trying to earn your love and acceptance by my performance. I give up on myself and accept the truth from God's Word that I am already accepted because I am in you, in Christ. I give up trying to earn others' approval, especially Nick's. I have failed miserably at that, and I know now that it is only what you do through me that will have any meaning. Thank you that you loved me enough to die for me. Amen."

Dr. Campbell gave Sara a book entitled *Blessings of Brokenness* by Charles Stanley and assigned it for her next appointment. Sara left his office that day with the assurance of God's love and acceptance.

7

The Fruit of Brokenness

Sara answered her cell phone. "Hello," she said.

"Sara, this is Nick. I need to see the kids. Can I take them this weekend? My mom and dad want to see them."

"Let me talk to them and see if they have any activities already scheduled. If not, I guess that would be okay. I know your parents miss them and haven't seen them since we've been separated. Would you like to come for dinner on Friday night before they go with you?"

There was a long silence on the other end of the phone. "I think that'd be all right. I'd like to make things seem as normal as possible for Madison and Michael," said Nick. "I guess I could come for dinner."

Sara breathed a sigh of relief. She had been praying that God would give her an opportunity to talk to Nick, and this seemed like just that.

Sara opened the door and saw Nick standing before her. He looked different than she had ever seen him. He was haggard, his face drawn and sad. He looked down at his feet, avoiding her eyes.

"Come in, Nick." She turned and hollered up the stairs. "Michael, Madison, your father's here."

The teenagers appeared at the top of the stairs. "Hi, Dad," they said.

Nick smiled and said, "Hi, you two. Boy, it's good to see you. I've really missed you both."

The twins bounded down the steps and hugged Nick. Madison began to cry.

"I've missed you so much. How are you?"

"Better, now that I see you both."

Sara wiped a tear from her eye and turned away. She was surprised at the emotional reunion.

"Come and sit down, Nick. I have dinner ready. Would you like to wash up first?"

Nick hesitated, not knowing how to respond to Sara's kindness. "Yes, I know where the powder room is. Thanks."

After dinner Sara said, "Madison and Michael, I'd like to talk to your father alone. Go upstairs and do your homework, and I'll call you when it's time to go."

Nick shifted nervously in his seat, not sure of what was coming. "I don't know if that's such a good idea. I really came just to pick up the kids."

"I think we need to talk," said Sara. "I promise that I won't get upset." She could feel Nick's trepidation.

Madison and Michael excused themselves, hugged Nick, and climbed the stairs.

"Let's listen to what they're saying," said Michael to his sister.

"No, that wouldn't be right, and, besides, I don't want to hear them fight. Let's do what Mom says so we can be ready to go with Dad."

Michael stared at his sister and thought, *Boy, this church thing must be working on her. She's not fighting Mom, which is not like her at all.*

God was at work in everyone, including the twins.

The Confession

Sara walked to the living room sofa and beckoned for Nick to join her. Haltingly, he walked from the dining room and sank down into the sofa. He longed to let it swallow him up and disappear.

"Nick, I want to tell you something, and I hope you will believe me. I have realized that I have been a very angry woman. In fact, I know now that I've been angry and fearful since I've been a little girl. There are a lot of things that caused it, which I have never told you, but that is no excuse. I know that I have not treated you with love and respect, and that I have shown you a lot of anger for things that were never your fault. I've learned from my counselor that once a person is angry, you pretty much get angry about everything and no one can do anything right. I have taken my anger out on you, and I am so sorry. I have never seen what a blessing you have been in my life, and I'm sorry for that. God has shown me my sin in being a controlling wife, and I need to ask for your forgiveness."

Nick sat speechless, not knowing what to say.

"I know you weren't expecting this. I'm sure you came with your guard up, but I pray that you have heard what I've said. I am ready and willing to change, and I want our marriage to work. I also know that only God can change me, and I want him to work in my life. Asking for your forgiveness is my first step. Please think about what I've said. No pressure. I just wanted you to know what's in my heart. I love you, Nick, and I'm so sorry for all the unkind things I've said and done."

Sara waited for Nick's response. *I hope he'll forgive me*, she thought.

Nick rose from the sofa, walked to the stairs, and called the kids so they could leave. Turning to Sara, he said, "I don't feel anything for you anymore. I don't feel love. I feel nothing. I think it's too late for us to get the love back that we once had. Numbness is all I feel for you. The only love I feel is for our kids."

"Nick, we can get it back. I am so sorry I've treated you badly. I know that God doesn't want our marriage to end."

"I'm not sure we were ever supposed to marry in the first place," he said. "After all, we weren't Christians, so how do we know that God wanted us to get married?"

"Because we are Christians now, and God has saved us both. I believe he wants to save our marriage, too. Can we at least try?"

"You've given me a lot to think about. I need time, to be by myself, and to think."

"Nick, would you please pray and ask God to help you to forgive me?"

"I don't think I'm there yet, and I don't know if I can get there."

"No, you can't get there by yourself, I know that. God has to get us there. We don't have the strength or the power to forgive on our own."

"I don't know what's happened to you, but you are not the same person I've been living with for the past sixteen years. I wish I could have that kind of faith."

"Nick, we've both accepted Christ as our Savior and Lord. He's here for a whole lot more than making sure we go to heaven when we die. He wants to enable us to change, forgive, and to live this life here on earth differently than we have been living. He is loving, and he can work on us to give us his kind of love for each other. Please, just don't give up on us. My counselor, Dr. Campbell, has been teaching me these things about God."

"I will think about what you've said, but I'm not sure we can get any love back. I can't stay in this marriage if I don't love you anymore. I've stayed for the kids, but that's over."

"Okay, Nick. I'll wait to hear from you."

Nick stared at Sara, thinking that *waiting* is something Sara's never done. *What is going on?*

"Michael, Madison, let's go. I'm ready, and Nana and Poppy are waiting for us at the house. Be sure you have everything you need for the weekend."

He turned to Sara and said, "Thanks for not making this difficult. I was anticipating a fight. I'll call when it's time for me to bring them home."

"That's okay, Nick. Just call me on my cell. I will be at church Sunday morning."

"Do you want me to take them to church on Sunday?" he said.

"That would be great. They both enjoy their Sunday school class, although Madison seems to like it a lot more than Michael, but he's coming around. It would be good for them to have you take them, if that's all right."

"I'll see what my mom and dad have planned, but again, thanks for not blowing up at me."

Madison and Michael walked down the stairs with their backpacks over their shoulders.

"Go back up and get some clothes for church, just in case we can make it this weekend," said their father.

"Really?" said Madison.

"Yes, really."

"Aww, Dad," said Michael.

"Just listen," said Nick.

"Okay," Michael said.

Nick gathered up the twins and their gear and walked down the sidewalk to his car. Sara watched from the door.

"Thank you, Lord, that Nick listened. Please give me strength to be patient and wait for him."

Surrender

During their next session, Dr. Campbell explained the "other side of the cross" to Sara, that when Jesus Christ died on the cross for her he was crucified for her, but she was also crucified "in" him. He explained the meaning of Galatians 2:20 and what her being crucified with Christ could mean for her life.

"Sara, Galatians 2:20 says that you were crucified with Christ and you no longer live, but Christ lives in you, and the life you now live in your body you live by faith in the Son of God who loved you and gave himself for you. Let me unpack that for you. When you in faith believed upon Christ's death, burial, and resurrection for your sins, God took you out of the dead, sinful life in Adam and placed you into the life of Christ. When he did that, his crucifixion became your co-crucifixion with Jesus. You died on the cross with him, according to this scripture, were buried with him, and rose from the dead with him. What was crucified on the cross with Jesus? Your old man, the person you were before you believed. According to Romans 6, your old man is the 'I' of Galatians 2:20 who was crucified. So, if you were crucified, who was that person?"

"I guess it was the terrible sinner, the angry me who couldn't hold her temper. Does that mean that all that I was before I became a Christian was crucified with Jesus on his cross?"

"Yes, that's exactly what it means. That Sara was also the one who was sexually abused, terrified, and unforgiving. She died with Jesus when he died, was buried with him when he was buried, and came out of the tomb with him as a new creation, totally new. Your sins were paid for, and they were left on that cross. The fact that Jesus Christ now lives in you and has given you his life enables you to forgive those who have hurt you, including David. That little girl who was abused, and the angry adult she became is dead. It is Christ living in you now who wants to live through you, not that angry woman. Do you think you can surrender your right to be angry with your abuser and use your anger to punish others, especially Nick, and even yourself?"

"I have to let it sink in that I died on the cross with Jesus. I have felt for several weeks that I'm dying, and now I know that

God has been putting to death that old me in the here and now. I must let her die. I really don't want that old me hanging around to rear her ugly head."

"She's already dead," said Dr. Campbell. "You must believe that in faith, and act accordingly. She died on the cross with Jesus, and the new Sara in Christ isn't angry and unforgiving, because that is not who Jesus is in and through you. Are you ready to surrender your rights to God?"

"I'm ready, but I need help."

"The Holy Spirit is in you to give you all that you need," he said. "Just pray this prayer after me."

"Dear Jesus, today I surrender my rights to you. I believe that I have been crucified with you on the cross and the old Sara is dead. I give up my right today to hold onto that angry woman I have been. I give up the right to stay angry with both my abuser, my father, and Nick."

Sara repeated the prayer and halted when Dr. Campbell mentioned her father; then she realized that not only was she angry with David but also all the men in her life, including her father. She continued the prayer.

"Yes, Lord, I give up my right to be angry with David, Nick, and my father. I need you to work in me so I can let it all go and forgive them. I'm ready, and I'm tired of carrying all this unforgiveness inside of me. I want it to go and have it gone for good."

"I want you to picture the cross of Christ, Sara, and Jesus standing in front of his cross in his long flowing white robe. Beside you stands David, the young man who sexually abused you. I want you to turn to him and tell him everything you've carried inside you since you were six years old."

Sara gulped, swallowed hard, and began to speak as if David were sitting next to her. Her eyes were closed as she was picturing the scene.

"David, you stole something from me and replaced it with a horrible fear. For years I've dreamed about you and have been filled with not only fear but also hatred of you. That sounds silly, because I don't even know if you're alive or dead. I hate you, David, for what you did to me. I know it made me afraid of men and that it affected my marriage to Nick. You ruined my life, and I hate you."

"Sara, can you take all that hatred out of your heart and put it in Jesus's hands, his hands with the nail scars on them? He suffered and died for David's sin against you, and he died for your hatred of him. I want you to picture a jar of black sludge, like dirty oil from a car. It's inside of you, and it is blocking God's love. Can you take that jar of sin—of hatred, fear, and unforgiveness—and put it in Jesus's hands?"

"Okay, I'll try. Jesus, I reach into my heart and get this big, black jar of sludge, of sin, all my hatred and unforgiveness. I give it to you, Jesus, because I know you died for it all. You shed your blood for every one of David's sins, and for my sins, too. I have been angry at David, but also at myself for allowing it to happen. I give you all my sin and my guilt, and I ask you to take them from me."

"Now, Sara, can you turn to David and forgive him?"

"Yes, I'm ready. David, I forgive you for hurting me. Jesus has forgiven me, and I forgive you in the name of the Lord Jesus Christ."

"Sara, by holding unforgiveness towards David, you've kept him in a prison inside of you. I want you to reach down, open the door of the jail cell, and set him free. Release him to Jesus and let Jesus have him."

"David, I have kept you in a prison inside my heart. I reach down now and open the jail cell. I set you free, and I give you to Jesus. I pray that you will know him and his forgiveness in your life. You are free, free from me now."

Sara looked up and smiled. "I saw the cell door open, and David walked out. Jesus was there, and he took him. David's gone."

"Are you afraid of him?"

"No, that's funny. For the first time, I'm not afraid of him. It feels like a warm blanket has just covered me."

"That's the peace of the Holy Spirit. He enabled you to forgive David and set him free. You are now free from David and your hatred of him. That's one of the reasons Jesus died for you and gave you his Spirit. Only he could bring healing from the abuse and freedom in forgiving David."

That night, Sara slept without the nightmare she had experienced since she was six years old.

8

My Husband Is My Father?

"I think I've figured out why I get so angry with Nick when he tells me he's leaving town with his job," Sara said to Dr. Campbell as they began their next counseling session.

"Really, and why is that?" Dr. Campbell responded.

"It's because my dad was never home, and I barely ever saw him. I had no relationship with him, and I didn't think he wanted to be close to me. I don't remember having conversations with him at all."

"So, is it possible that when Nick says he needs to travel because of his work, a button gets pushed inside your mind that takes you back to your childhood when your dad would leave, too?"

"I suppose so. Yes, you're right."

"How do you feel when you think of your father not being home and having a father-daughter relationship with you?"

"Sad and hurt. Like I didn't count. I never felt I mattered to him."

"If I asked you now to reach down into your heart and pull up the feelings you have about your relationship with him, what would you find?"

"Hurt, feelings of rejection, and some anger. A lot of anger. That surprises me, because I've never thought I was an angry person. I've always gotten my feelings hurt so easily."

"Would it surprise you to know that hurt feelings can turn into anger if you don't know how to release them to the Lord?" said Dr. Campbell.

"No, because I have been very angry with Nick because of his job. And I know I'm angry with my father, and he died several years ago."

"Do you remember when we talked about the fact that Jesus accepts you just as you are because he has chosen you and put you into Christ—acceptance based upon him and his love and not upon what you do? Do you remember?"

"Yes, I do," said Sara.

"Well, that's the basis for releasing the feelings of rejection you've experienced from your father, and then again from Nick every time he wasn't there for you and the twins. Jesus will never reject you, and you must look to him for your acceptance and not to your father, Nick, or anyone else. When we can give all those feelings of hurt and rejection to the Lord, the next step will be to release the anger and unforgiveness towards them both."

"It's so amazing to me that I have pinned my father's behavior on Nick, probably all my married life, and then rejected him for it. I've felt rejected, but then I have rejected, too. I've been pretty nasty to Nick. I've pushed him away. I can see that now."

"It's a good thing when God shows us our own sin, because the next step is confessing it and repenting of it. Repentance means a change of direction in our lives. You have lived your whole life feeling rejected by your father and carried that over to Nick. Now, in repentance you make a decision not to take their absence as a personal rejection of you. It's not about you. It's about what God wants you to believe about him and his place in your life."

"Wow, it's hard for me to believe that I've been unhappy for this many years because of things that happened to me as a child. Have I done this all to myself?"

"This is what sin does, Sara. It separates us from God first and then from others in our relationships. When we base who we are upon what others think of us, or upon the attention others do or do not pay to us, we will always be disappointed. No one can ever give us the perfect love and acceptance that God can, so we will always come up lacking."

"So, what's next?" said Sara.

"I want you to go home and write two letters, one to Nick and one to your father. In it say everything that you have carried in your heart against them, every time they weren't there for you, every time you felt like they didn't care. Write it all out and speak to them, just as if each one were sitting on this couch next to you, and then come back ready to forgive during your next appointment. I also want you to listen to a recording by Malcolm Smith on forgiveness. It's one of the best teachings I've heard on the subject, and I think it will really help you with this process."

Sara rose with both excitement and anxiety, but she knew she was moving forward toward the goal of health in her soul. "Beloved, I pray that all may go well with you and that you may be in good health, as it goes well with your soul" (3 John 1:2).

Dear ...

Sara sat on her bed with legs crossed and pen and notebook in hand.

"How do I start?" she said. "There've been so many years and a bushel of hurts. It seems silly to write a letter to my father, because he's gone. I can't keep procrastinating. I have to do it. My appointment with Dr. Campbell is in two days, so I don't have much time."

She wrote on the paper, "Dear Dad."

At first, she wrote slowly, as if she were searching for the perfect words. Then, as the pen picked up speed, the words flowed, and her tears spilled out upon the paper.

Dad, every time I looked into the audience or the grandstand when I received an award, played a sport, or graduated from high school, I hoped I would see your face, but you weren't there. Never. Mom always made excuses for you, but I knew that it just didn't matter to you. Other things, your business, your customers, were always more important. You could have spared an hour or two. I never heard an 'I'm sorry I wasn't there, Sara.' I knew I wasn't important enough for you to make time for me. I never felt like I belonged to you. I was out there on my own without any help from anyone in my family. I looked for you, but I never saw you. You were the epitome of the absentee father. I'm angry with you because I never knew you. The boys and Jane worked for you, so you paid attention to them, although you were hard on the boys. I couldn't do that. I was too young, so I didn't exist. And then you died, and I didn't feel anything. I took care of all your affairs and of Mom, too, because you left everything disorganized. I was smart enough to do that, but not good enough for you to give me any of your attention. You had a favorite child, and I wasn't it. Why did you do that? It set up such jealousy and hard feelings in the family. A parent should never have a favorite child, but you did. You were all about your work, and I didn't fit. I was smart in school, but that was never important to you. You never congratulated me or said you were proud of me for anything. I hate you, Dad, and I'm so sorry I have those feelings. I don't like having them, but why did you even have me if you didn't want me? I know I have to get rid of all these terrible feelings toward you. You are gone now and in heaven, and I'm sure this would upset you if you knew how I felt, but really, Dad, did you think you were a good father to me? You thought that if you provided money, then that was enough. I didn't expect you to give me money. I just wanted to know the love of a father. I believe I really missed out on that, and now I know it affected my marriage. I don't want to blame you or be angry, so I need to let you go.

"Whew," said Sara. "That was hard. I had no idea I had all that inside my heart. Now, it's time to write the letter to Nick."

Dear Nick, I've known you since college days, and I've loved you since we first met. I've often thought that I might not have married you if I would have known you would spend our marriage in a traveling job. That's not true, and I know that, because I've never loved anyone else. I confess to you that I have looked at your job and your going away from home as a personal rejection of me and the kids, not as something you had to do. I've built up feelings of hurt, rejection, and anger in my heart towards you for years, since the first day of our marriage. Then, during our first year of marriage when you were away and I had a miscarriage of our baby, I was upset beyond belief. You left me and went to another state, and while you were gone, I lost the baby. You never understood what I went through without you there, and I was very young and needed you with me. I have not forgiven you for that, and now I know I need to forgive and give my anger to the Lord. I have hated your job, your boss, and everything that pulled you away from me. Every time you went away and missed something important going on at home, the anger piled on until I could hardly be civil to you. I have seethed with anger towards you at times, and I know you couldn't understand why I acted the way I did. I believe God has allowed me to suffer migraine headaches as a way of making me deal with my anger. I pray that our relationship can become healthy, and that we can love each other again. I confess my anger to the Lord, and I ask him and you, Nick, to forgive me for it. I choose to forgive you for the job that you have and for not being with me when I had the miscarriage. I forgive you for every day that you were gone, and I ask God to forgive me for the way I have treated you. I set you free to be who God created you to be, and I accept you and the job that you have as gifts from God. I want God to teach me to love you the way a Christian wife should love her husband. Please forgive me, Nick.

Letting Go

"Are you ready?" said Dr. Campbell as he finished his opening prayer.

"Yes, I believe so."

"Okay, let me see what you wrote."

He took her letters, looked over them, and handed them back to her.

"Okay, Sara. I want you to take your letter to your father and read it as a prayer. Picture your father sitting beside you here, and say to him what you need to say."

Sara took the letter and began to read. Her voice quivered, and as she came to the end, the emotional chains fell.

"I forgive you, Daddy. I'm sorry we never knew each other, but I choose not to hold that against you anymore. I cancel the debt that I have held against you my whole life. Please forgive me, Lord Jesus, for hating my father. I forgive him and set him free from the prison I've held him in within my heart."

"Okay, Sara, now let's read the letter to Nick and forgive him."

Sara read the letter to Nick, and afterwards, she wiped her tears away from her face and smiled.

"They're free, both of them, and I can feel the weight leaving my body. There's a peace inside that I have never had. Thank you, Dr. Campbell."

"Don't thank me," he said. "Thank our Lord Jesus Christ. He did it for you and in you."

"Do you think Nick will come home and our marriage will make it?" said Sara.

"I don't know," said Dr. Campbell. "Just because you've forgiven Nick doesn't mean he'll automatically come home, or that your marriage will be saved. Forgiveness is between you and God, and we do it because God commands it. It is for our own good that we release the prisoners we hold inside our hearts, but there are no guarantees that the other person will change or also forgive us. I can't promise that. Only God knows what is going to happen, and all we can do is pray that Nick will see a change in you and realize you are not the angry wife you have been to him."

"I asked God to teach me to love Nick. I don't know if I've ever really loved him the way I should. I feel like I need to start our marriage over again."

"Perhaps you're right. You are a new believer in Christ, and only he can give you the love you need to have to love your husband unselfishly. We are all self-centered without Christ, and we live looking to our mates to meet our needs, take care of us, put us first, and a hundred other things. Jesus can teach us how to deny ourselves and think of others before ourselves. That is what Jesus did for us when he hung on that cross and gave his life for us. He put us and our salvation before his own life, and only he can replace our selfishness with unconditional love for our mates. He is at work in you, so be patient with what he's doing in your life. It's a huge thing that you were able to forgive your father and Nick today, and I believe there will be good consequences from that."

"I am determined to treat Nick differently. Do you think I can?"

"Jesus is in you, through the power of his Holy Spirit, and you need to remember to call upon him when you are faced with a difficult situation, such as when you see Nick. Just shoot up what I call 'arrow prayers' to God by praying something like this, 'Jesus, I don't want to react or overreact without thinking. Please love Nick through me and teach me to accept him the way he is.'"

"That sounds good," said Sara. "Arrow prayers. I like that. I need to remember that. It's like an emergency prayer."

"You can talk to God anytime," said Dr. Campbell. "It doesn't have to be a formal prayer, or when you are on your knees or in church. God is your very best friend, your father or daddy, and he wants you to talk to him all day, just as you would to your best friend. Let me show you a scripture in the Bible. 1 Thessalonians says, 'Pray without ceasing.' That means pray all the time, anytime, night or day. God wants us to do that so you can reach out to him for help. This is a new discipline for you, so I want you to try to do that this upcoming week. I believe God will bless you as a result. You'll be bringing him into areas of your life in which you never thought about turning to God."

"This is such a change in how I've lived my life," said Sara. "I never thought God was interested in the details of my life. I've always believed that he cared only about the big things, like when someone's sick or dying. Is he really concerned about everything in my life?"

"Are you concerned?" said Dr. Campbell.

"Yes," said Sara.

"Then he's concerned," he said. "He cares about everything that concerns you."

"Okay, I'll try that this week. The first thing I'll pray about is my marriage."

9

It's Nick's Turn

Sara opened the front door and was surprised to see Nick on the porch.

"Hi," he said, "I hope you won't be mad, but my boss gave me these tickets to the hockey game for tonight, and I was hoping the twins could go with me."

"You're in luck," she answered. "It's spring break, and they have nothing planned. In fact, they were just complaining that they're bored. Let me go and get them."

Within minutes, Madison and Michael ran down the stairs, greeted their father, and headed toward the car. Nick's face showed an air of incredulity.

"Have them back tonight, but no hurry," cried Sara after them.

Nick settled in behind the steering wheel and collected his thoughts before starting the car. *Wow, that was easier than I thought it would be. I fully expected a fight and that Sara would say no. I guess she has changed.*

"Gee, Dad, this is great! I'm excited to see my favorite team play. I was beginning to think we weren't going to have any fun this spring break."

"Yeah, I know," answered Nick. "It used to be our special time to take family vacations."

"Maybe we can get back to doing that again," said Madison.

Nick was silent and didn't respond, but he rolled Madison's words over in his mind.

Weeks later, Sara answered her cell phone, "Hello."

"Hi," said Nick. "Could you do me a favor?"

"Sure," she said.

"Could you give me the name of the counselor you've been seeing?"

"Yes. His name is Dr. Ryan Campbell, and he's located in the professional building behind the hospital."

"Okay, thanks," said Nick.

That was all he said, but it was enough. Sara dropped to her knees and started to cry.

"Oh, God. Thank you, thank you. Maybe there's hope for our marriage. Please give Nick the courage to see Dr. Campbell."

The Appointment

"Mr. Antonio, come in," said Dr. Campbell, as he opened his office door.

Nick crossed the room and settled into the brown, butter-soft leather couch. He surveyed the office with a sweeping glance, absorbing the golf course pictures and the myriad of diplomas on the doctor's wall.

Dr. Campbell saw Nick staring at the Amen Corner picture of the Augusta National and said, "So, do you play golf?"

"Yes, although I rarely have the time. I had wanted to teach my son to play, but that never happened."

"Well, maybe you still can. It's never too late to learn to play golf. I like to get out at night, even if it's just for a few holes."

"Sounds nice, but my life has been so upside down lately that golf is the last thing on my mind."

"Why don't you tell me about it?" said Dr. Campbell. "Why is your life upside down?"

"My wife and I are separated, but I guess you already know that. I don't know what to tell you and what not to tell you."

"Let's start from the beginning and assume that I don't know anything about you. When a person comes in for counseling, I look at it as an opportunity for me to lead that person to allow God to work in his life. That's it. This isn't for your wife or to fix her or blame her. This time is for you to get whatever help and counsel you need for your life."

"That sounds good. I feel like I've been going in circles, not knowing where I'm going to end up. I thought my marriage was over, but now I'm not sure. I'm not sure about much of anything. I guess I'm just confused about my life in general."

"Tell me, Nick, what do you believe about God, or do you believe in God?"

"Yes, I do, although that is a recent thing."

"Then what do you believe about Jesus Christ? Who is he to you?"

"A friend of mine told me that he died on the cross to forgive me of my sins. I believe that, but I think that's about all I know."

"Great, then that's where we'll start, with Jesus. Do you believe that he's God?"

"I don't understand all of that. Why is there God and then Jesus? Why isn't there just God?"

"Let's look at the first chapter of the book of John."

Dr. Campbell picked up a Bible, opened it, and said, "Nick, would you please read the first few verses?"

"In the beginning was the Word, and the Word was with God, and the Word was God. He was in the beginning with God. All things were made through him, and without him was not any thing made that was made" (John 1:1–3).

"Nick, another name for the Word is Jesus Christ, and knowing that, what does what you just read say?"

"It says that Jesus was in the beginning with God, and Jesus was God. It also says that nothing was made without him. That's amazing to me. Did he make everything?"

"Yes, that's what the Bible says. He and God are the same. They are the same person. That is what we call the Trinity, and the third person of the Trinity is the Holy Spirit. Father, Son, and Holy Spirit. The first, second, and third persons of the Trinity, all co-equal, and all God. Each one, according to the Bible, has a different function, but each is God. God is our Father, Jesus Christ is the Son who came to earth in human form to die for us, and the Holy Spirit is the one Jesus left behind when He ascended into heaven after his death, burial, and resurrection. The Holy Spirit's job is to teach us about Jesus through the Bible and the scriptures. He bears witness to Jesus. I'll give you some scriptures to read at home this coming week to show you these truths."

"Okay, that would be good."

"Nick, are you open to allowing God to change your life through what we do here?"

"Yes, I've noticed a huge change in Sara, and I want to be open to change. It's hard, though, because I don't know what that will look like. I've been like this all my life, and I think I've really messed things up at home. I don't know how to be different."

"You aren't the one who will make you different. God will work in your life through his Holy Spirit. God knows what you need, and he knows you inside out. Are you willing to trust him with your life and your future?"

"Yes, I think so, although I am a little afraid to do that."

"He understands that, and he will take you one step at a time. Proverbs 3:5-6 says 'Trust in the Lord with all your heart, and do not lean on your own understanding. In all your ways acknowledge him, and he will make straight your paths.' Can you tell God that you're willing to trust him with your life?"

"I think so," said Nick.

"Good, then would you like to pray and ask God to be in charge of your life?"

"Okay, but I think I'd like to do it by myself, if that's all right with you."

Getting back to his apartment, Nick made a cup of coffee, poured some cream into it, and sat down, all the while thinking about Dr. Campbell's words: *God knows what you need; he'll take you one step at a time. He understands.*

I've never thought of God like that, but I believe Dr. Campbell knows what he's talking about. I certainly have made a mess of things. My marriage is coming apart, and I wake up every day with a heaviness inside, not able to figure out what to do. He said that God would guide me. I've got nothing to lose, except maybe a lot of confusion. He set down his coffee mug, slid off the chair, and knelt beside it.

"God, I want to give you my life and everything in it—Sara, the kids, my job, everything—but I am afraid. Help me with my fear. I've always been in control of where I go and what I do, and I don't know how not to do that. Will you please help me to change and to be a better husband and father? I believe I've missed a lot of my kids' lives, and I want to have a Christian family, whatever that means. I want to let go of all I can with your help. Jesus, thank you that you died for my sins. I do believe that, and I have to believe that you died for all my screw-ups, too. I need you, God."

Nick stood up and felt almost a giddiness rising inside his chest, along with relief. "Wow, I feel so much better. That's amazing!"

He called Sara.

"Hello," she said.

"Hi, are you busy? Can I come over?"

"Of course."

"I'll be there in twenty minutes or so."

Nick rang the bell and waited. As Sara opened the door, he blurted out, "I'd like to come home."

Sara didn't say anything, but the tears welling up in her eyes told her response. She stepped forward and extended her hand to her husband.

"I've been praying, Nick, that you'd come home and that God would save our marriage. I want you to be here with me and the kids. I know that with God's help we can make it."

Nick crossed the threshold of his house, and for the first time in a long time, he was home.

The Healing

During their next appointment, Dr. Campbell asked Nick, "Can you help me to get to know your father?"

"There's not much to know. He didn't talk much, especially to me. He fought in the war, and I didn't see him until I was two years old. My mother told me I would never let him hold me, because I lived with her and my grandmother and wasn't used to men. He worked all the time, holidays too, and was not home much when I was growing up."

"Did your dad ever teach you anything, like how to drive, or how to play a sport?"

"No, my uncle taught me to drive. My dad was always too busy with his job."

"How did that make you feel?"

"I never thought about how it made me feel. I don't think about feelings much. In fact, I have a hard time feeling emotion most of the time."

"How do you think you felt about him when you were growing up?"

"He was a stranger to me, because I hardly ever saw him."

"Do you remember him holding you on his lap, reading you a story, or putting you to bed?"

"No. He was gone when I got up in the morning and wasn't home by the time I went to bed. I don't remember him when I was growing up. He was a partner with his brothers in a business, and that was the most important thing to him. Working was his life, and I guess I wasn't part of that."

"Now, Nick, how does that make you feel?"

"Pretty left out and unimportant, like he didn't care enough to be there."

"Can you tell me about your mother?"

"Very emotional, high-strung. That's the best way I can describe her. I stayed away from her a lot, because she was always on an emotional roller coaster. I didn't know how to handle that, so I just closed her off. I spent most of my time outside, playing sports in the street with my friends."

"Who in your life has reminded you of your mother?"

"Sara. Oh my gosh, that's true."

"How would you describe her?"

"Emotional and high-strung, although she's changing."

"And how have you handled that?"

"I haven't. I guess I've closed her off, too."

"Why do you think that is?"

"Maybe because my mother was like that. I can see the parallel now. Whenever Sara would get upset, I would walk away or leave. I shut down."

"Was showing emotion in your parents' home always a bad thing, something unpleasant to steer clear of?"

"Yes, it was either yelling or crying. There wasn't a whole lot of laughter. My mom was usually mad about something, and a lot of the time, I had no idea why, so I stayed away from it."

"How have you dealt with Sara's migraine headaches?"

"I haven't. Sometimes I've tried to help, when I'm home, but I've felt pretty useless. I've stayed away from her, because I never knew what to expect when I came home."

"What about your kids? How have you gotten along with them?"

"They are closer to their mother than they are to me, but I guess that's natural. I know they resent me because of my job. They've had to move and change schools so many times. They're angry with me, although I think they're relieved that I've come home. I'm not sure, though."

"Have you always traveled with your job?"

"Yes."

"Have there been times when you went away just to remove yourself from the circumstances at home?"

"Yes, although I never thought about that. I guess I was wrong to do that. My job hasn't been stressful like my home life."

"Have you ever thought that your job has provided stress to your family, since you've uprooted them so many times from schools and friends?"

"No, I always thought of our moves as good things, opportunities to see new places and meet new people."

"That might be true for some adults, those who don't need to make lasting friendships or have stability in school life, but it is very difficult for children to move around so much, no matter what age they are. Someday you might want to have a conversation with your children about that and how they have felt and coped with the moves."

Nick sat and thought about Madison and Michael.

"It has just dawned on me that I don't know my kids very well, just like my dad didn't know me. We've taken some vacations together, but that's about it. I don't spend much time with them. Do you think they resent me for that?"

"I don't know, but it might be something you need to ask them. Asking them for forgiveness for all the time you've been away and for uprooting them so many times would be in order. It could bring about some healing in your relationship with them."

"I've never thought about asking for forgiveness, because I didn't think I did anything wrong. But now I see that my job choices have been tough on my family. I will ask them to forgive me. I've told them that my job left me no choice but to move."

"Nick, there are always choices in life. You've made the decision to allow God to make the choices for you now, right?"

"Do you think he doesn't want me to have the job that I have now?"

"I don't know, but if you place that decision in his hands, he'll do what's best for you and your family."

Nick got into his car and sat motionless behind the steering wheel. Dr. Campbell's last words flooded his mind: *He'll do what's best for you and your family.*

"Please, God," Nick whispered. "Show me what to do. I want my family back."

The Twins

Nick sat at the dinner table as Sara put the food on the table. The twins were called for dinner, but they didn't respond. Since he had come home, they had become more and more distant. He didn't know if he was doing something wrong, or if they weren't happy that he and Sara had reconciled. Whatever the reason, he sensed a wall between them that was getting worse by the day.

As Madison and Michael entered the dining room, Nick said, "How was school today, guys?"

"Okay, I guess," Madison said.

Michael said nothing, pulled the chair out from the table, and sat down half-heartedly.

"Michael, how are you doing?" said Nick.

He glanced up sullenly, and then lowered his eyes to his iPhone.

"Michael, I asked you a question, and I expect an answer."

"Since when do you deserve an answer? Just because you've come back home doesn't mean that you're all of a sudden a supergreat father. I've done okay without you for a long time, and I really don't need you anymore."

Nick's stomach churned at Michael's words. *How can I ever repair this?* he thought.

"Michael, what can I do to make things better between us?"

"Nothing," he said. "It's too late. I'll be gone soon, so it doesn't matter."

Michael and Madison would be graduating from high school in a few years and Nick prayed that it was not too late to repair his relationships with them.

Nick dropped the subject because he could feel the wall getting thicker. He didn't know where all Michael's anger started, but all of a sudden, it was bigger than both of them. If Nick had learned anything from Dr. Campbell, it was that he couldn't make anything happen by himself. Only God could.

Please, God, help us love each other again. I need to ask them for forgiveness, but I know they won't listen now. Open the door for me to be able to talk to them.

Sara and Nick ate dinner in relative silence, and Madison and Michael retired to their room to do their homework as soon as they finished dinner.

"Sara, will you forgive me for all the times I've made you move with my job? I've never seen it from your point of view, how hard it was for you to pull up stakes and start over in a new city."

"I already have, Nick," she said, "but, yes, I forgive you."

"I'm sure there are a lot of things I've done wrong in our marriage. I don't know them all, but would you forgive me for all the times I was insensitive and didn't understand what you needed? I've been on my own success track and just expected you and the kids to follow me. I know that was unfair."

"Nick, it made me feel like my opinion didn't count. You would come home and tell me we were moving, not asking me how I felt about it or even if I wanted to move. You made the decision, and the kids and I didn't have any say. Our lives were affected, too, but it seemed to us that it didn't matter to you. You acted like your job was the most important thing to you, and we didn't count."

"I know it must've seemed that way to you, but you always mattered. I just didn't know how to show it. Will you forgive me?"

"Yes."

"I know the kids are mad at me. Michael especially doesn't seem at all happy that I'm home. I don't know what to do about that."

"We have to pray, Nick. We can't make him or even help him to forgive you. I think Michael is still trying to decide what he believes about Jesus Christ. This has all been very tough for him. Madison seems to have a much more tender heart towards God. I don't know if she's angry, but I think she will forgive you if you ask her. Michael is the more distant one. He holds everything in, just like you, so it's hard to know what he's thinking. He is his father's son, showing very little emotion, and you have to pry things out of him. He's more difficult to read."

"Well, I have my work cut out for me," said Nick.

"I just think we need to take it one day at a time. We don't really know how to be together as a family, because you've always been away so much. It's been the kids and me most of their lives. We have to show them that we're changing, although I know I will still make mistakes and sin. I'm not perfect, and I can't try to be. We need to ask God to change us into the mom and dad that our kids need now. I don't want to lose our kids when they go off to college. We have only a little time left that they'll be home with us."

"I want our home life to change, Sara. I've asked God to change me. I only hope our kids can forgive me."

"Give them time," she said.

The Letters

"Tell me about your week, Nick," said Dr. Campbell.

"I'm home now, and I tried not to travel this past week. Sara and I talked about the twins and their anger towards me, and we committed to pray for them, particularly Michael, because he is so angry."

"That's a very important step in this process, praying for forgiveness, both of yourself and from others. Did you write the letters that I asked you to write during our last appointment?"

"Yes, I did, although it was very difficult. I kept getting stuck, because I had a hard time writing down how I felt about my family—my mother and father, and then Sara. I wanted to give up many times, but I knew you wouldn't be happy if I didn't complete the assignment. I realized what an achiever I am, too, that I wanted to do a good job with the letters."

"You don't have to perform for me, Nick. You're not doing this for me, because the letters are between you and God. They are for you, because God commands us to forgive in Matthew. You cannot have peace and freedom in your relationships until you forgive, and the first people you must deal with are your parents. I'd like to read you the Bible verses where Jesus talks about forgiveness. In the Lord's Prayer, Jesus said, 'Forgive us our debts, as we also have forgiven our debtors' (Matt. 6:12). May I see the letters you've written?"

Nick took them from his Bible and handed them to Dr. Campbell.

"I want you to read them just as if you were standing in front of Jesus and his cross. Talk to your father and then to Jesus. At the end, you will forgive your dad."

Nick began to read:

Dear Dad, I can count on one hand the
number of conversations we had while I was

growing up. They were mostly about the store, the grocery orders, or what I did wrong with the delivery truck. You never sat down with me and talked to me about anything other than working for you. I didn't know you when I was young, because you were not home when I was awake. You worked at the store on holidays and came home exhausted, too tired to do anything with me or mom. We didn't have a father-son relationship, one in which a dad taught his son how to do things or what it was like to be a man. I missed out on a lot, because you didn't let me get to know you. You were always so quiet, and you didn't talk to me. I wondered what I did wrong, because you always acted like you were mad or just didn't want to talk to me. When I worked for you after school, you were harder on me than on any of the other employees. I had to do everything perfectly, and when I messed up you would yell. The store and the orders were more important than me. If you were sitting right here beside me, I would tell you that I never knew you, not really. I knew you as a taskmaster, a hard worker, but not as my father. I guess I loved you, but I don't feel love for you. I don't feel anything. You're a stranger that I wish I had known, and for that I am very sad. I believe our relationship has made it harder for me to relate to my own kids, because I don't know how to be a dad, or what I'm supposed to do in a marriage. Our home life was not happy during my childhood, and I blame you for that. As I write this, I realize how angry I am with you, and how that has affected my life. I've become just like you in a lot of ways, and I am angry. You were my model, and it wasn't a good one of a dad or a husband.

"Now, Nick, take your dad by the hand and lead him to the cross. See Jesus standing in front of the cross with his hands outstretched. I want you to confess your anger to Jesus and then turn and forgive your father."

"Jesus, I confess that I have been angry with my father for a long time. Please forgive me for my anger towards my father."

"Now, talk to your father and forgive him."

"Dad, I forgive you for not being there for me when I was growing up. I forgive you for being so demanding of me when I drove the truck for the store. I forgive you for not being the dad that I needed and not teaching me how to be a boy and a man. I forgive you for all those times that you weren't home, and for all the lonely days and nights. I forgive you that learning was not important to you and that I had to struggle so much in school. I forgive you for not helping me to learn anything, and for the fact that I've had to do it all by myself."

"Nick, inside your heart is a big jar of black sludge that is your anger and unforgiveness toward your father. Reach down inside your heart and take that jar of sin and hand it to Jesus."

"Lord Jesus, I reach down inside me and grab the jar of black sin, my anger and unforgiveness toward my father. I take it and put it in your hands, Lord. Please forgive me for all of it."

"Now, tell your father that you forgive him and let him go."

"Dad, I choose to forgive you because Jesus has forgiven me. I choose to let you go and to accept you just the way you are. You are free to be who God created you to be. You don't owe me anything, not an apology, nothing. I hope that I can know you at least a little bit in the years that we have left together."

"Nick, that was a big step in the forgiveness process. Can you see how your feelings towards your father have affected your life?"

"I think so. That's sad."

"Yes, but it's not too late for your relationship with your children to change. Let's ask God to work in them and you to know each other in a new way."

"Okay."

Nick bowed his head and prayed with Dr. Campbell.

"God, please change my relationship with my kids. Make us know each other and love each other. I don't want them to feel about me the way I've felt about my father. In Jesus name, Amen."

10

Sara's Sister, Jane

"Hello," droned Sara as she clumsily fumbled with the phone.

"Sara, what's wrong with you?" said her sister, Jane.

"I'm in bed with a migraine," she said.

"You're just like your mother," Jane said. "Always sick. Our mother does that for attention, and so do you."

The heat rose into Sara's face and head. Her heart pounded in her head until she felt like it would explode.

Thirteen years separated Jane and Sara. As a little girl, Sara tried to shut out the abusive language that Jane hurled at their mother. Home was a place where Jane treated others as if they were created to serve her, and her mother didn't escape that role. Jane ruled the home and those who lived there. Sara spent her adult life maintaining distance between her and her sister, primarily because of the way Jane treated her mother.

Sara often wondered when the anger and hatred had started in her family. It seemed to start with Jane and spread like a cancer through the family relationships. Sara's remedy was to back away from the angry people as a means of self-protection.

The Diagnosis

"Sara, I need a knee replacement to help me walk. The rheumatoid arthritis has affected my walking, and my doctor has recommended surgery. I need to bank some blood for myself, in case I need a transfusion. Could you come and donate blood for me?"

"Jane, I haven't talked to you for years, and I didn't know you had been diagnosed with RA. How long have you had it?" said Sara.

"For five years, and it has progressed very rapidly," said Jane. "My arms and legs have been drastically affected. I walk with a cane, and I'm very unsteady. I have a hard time writing now, and my life has become pretty difficult. Will you help me with blood for this surgery?"

"Let me pray about it first," said Sara. "Nick is away, and the twins are my responsibility. I also take care of Mother, you know, or, perhaps you didn't know that she lives nearby, now that Dad is gone."

Sara assumed that Jane wouldn't understand her need to pray about the decision, but she said it anyway. The sisters were strangers.

Isn't that just like Jane? thought Sara. *I haven't seen her for twenty years, and the only time she calls me is when she needs something. Still, she must be in pretty bad shape if she has a hard time walking. I'll have to talk to Nick and see if he can be in town in order for me to leave and go see her.*

Sara half-heartedly listened to Jane's voice complaining about not having anyone to help her, but she wasn't going to be guilted into making a decision. She had home responsibilities that had to be taken care of first.

"When is your surgery, and how soon would you need me to donate the blood?"

"It's a month away, and the blood can be given up to two weeks before that. So, you have a couple of weeks before you would have to come. I would love for you to be here, though, for my surgery."

Sara was incredulous at Jane's request, because she had never reached out to her before.

"I'll call you and let you know if I can come, after I talk to Nick. He travels all the time, and he would have to arrange his schedule so that he could be in town while I'm gone. We'll see if we can work that out."

Sara hung up the phone and poured a cup of coffee. She felt sorry for Jane, because she knew she had alienated most of the people in her life. Her marriage had ended in divorce, and she lived alone.

"What a tough place for her to be in," said Sara aloud. "Jane has been angry and difficult for years. Now she seems sad and helpless."

She spoke to Nick that evening by telephone. "Your sister? I haven't seen her since our wedding day. I didn't know she ever wanted anything to do with us. Has she had a change of heart?"

"I don't know," said Sara. "She needs help, and she said that the rheumatoid arthritis has taken a toll on her body. I feel sorry for her, and I would like to help her."

"Okay," said Nick. "If you want to go to help her, then I'll help you to do that. Perhaps you can mend your relationship with her. I know it's always been difficult for you because of your mother."

"Thanks so much, Nick," said Sara. "It means a lot to me that you're willing to help make this happen, although, to be honest, I am afraid of Jane. I remember her screaming and yelling at my mother when I was growing up. I was no match for her when she got like that. I hope that won't happen to me if I go to see her."

"If she treats you badly, then come home. I wish I could go with you, but that's impossible. I will need to be home at night for the twins and to be close by for your mother. I will pray for you and your visit."

Nick's offer to pray for her gave Sara a sense of peace. They had begun to communicate about their faith.

In a few weeks, Sara stood beside Jane's bed after her surgery. As she stared at her sister's face, her mind was deluged with memories of the abuse Jane had levied upon their mother.

I don't know this woman, she thought, and here I am giving blood for her. Fortunately, our blood types were a match. I trust God that he has a purpose in this, but I am a stranger here.

Sara had been a Christian for two years, and she spent much time reading her Bible and talking to God. Standing beside Jane's bed, she thought of some verses she had read.

'If a man curses his mother or his father, then he will surely die' (Mark 7:10). *'A tranquil heart gives life to the flesh, but envy makes the bones rot'* (Prov. 14:30).

The doctor had been in and had told her the condition of Jane's body. Her bones were like sawdust, and he didn't know if the screws used to secure the artificial knee would hold. Her bones, in actual fact, were deteriorating, or rotting.

As Sara paced back and forth around her sister's bed, she had a revelation. "It is because Jane hates my mother that her bones are rotting. I need to talk to her about Jesus Christ and his forgiveness of our sins."

A few days later, as Sara was reading her Bible and praying for Jane, she told her sister, "Jane, you are going to have to forgive Mother. Let me read you these verses from the Bible. 'If a man curses his mother or his father, then he will surely die.' 'A tranquil heart gives life to the flesh, but envy makes the bones rot.'"

"Jane," said Sara. "You must forgive our mother."

"Oh, please don't tell me that. That means I will never get well."

"Please let me help you to work towards being able to forgive Mother. I don't know why you hate her, but Jesus Christ died on the cross for your sins to forgive you, and he died for all of Mother's sins, too, no matter what has happened between the two of you. Whatever your reasons, Jesus can give you all that you need in order to forgive. He died for you, Jane, so you can be forgiven and know him as your Savior and Lord of your life. Do you believe that? Please turn to him and ask him for forgiveness of your sins, so that you can know him as your Heavenly Father."

Jane closed her eyes, and Sara stopped talking. She prayed silently for her sister, that she would accept God's grace into her life and believe that Jesus Christ paid the penalty for her sins, for everyone's, including their mother.

"Jane, I'm leaving in the morning for home."

Jane opened her eyes, and Sara looked into deep wells of fear.

"Please don't leave me," Jane said. "I am afraid I may never get better."

"I must go home to Michael and Madison, and Nick needs to get back to his traveling schedule. He has stayed in town with the kids so that I could come here to be with you."

"Please tell him how much I appreciate his doing that."

Sara was shocked to hear gratitude from Jane's lips. It was the first time her sister had willingly thought of someone other than herself, at least in Sara's recollection.

Death Knocks Once

R-r-r-ring, cried the landline as Sara rushed to catch it before the answering machine picked up.

"Aunt Sara?" the hushed voice said from the other end.

"Yes," Sara said.

"Mom's had a massive stroke," said Callie, Jane's grown daughter.

"Oh, no," said Sara. "How did that happen?"

"She decided to have a second surgery on her other knee to replace the left one, and she must've developed a blood clot that traveled to her brain. She's in critical condition."

"I am sorry, Callie. I will pray for her, but I cannot come right now. Your grandmother is in the hospital for surgery, and I must be here to take care of her. Will you please let me know what happens with your mom? I'm sorry I can't come, but I take care of my mother, and she is not well now."

Silence was the response, and the line went dead.

"I can't go to see her right now. I have to be here for Mother. Callie doesn't understand that. Jane has probably filled her mind with negative stories about her grandmother."

Death knocked once at the door of Jane's life that day, but Jane recovered from the stroke. It affected her speech and her walking but left her mind and memory intact. There were two more years during which the sisters spoke on the phone, and Sara often guided the conversation around to the subject of Jesus and his forgiveness and unconditional love.

"Sara, I asked Jesus to forgive me of my sins, and I believe that he did. I feel so much better, not physically, but I'm not as afraid as I was before," said Jane one day.

Sara was elated at the good news of her sister's acceptance of Christ and his salvation. "No matter what happens, Jane, you will be all right, because Jesus Christ lives in you and has given you his life. Your life will never end, even when you leave this earth, because he has given you eternal life, which is his life. You won't die, even though your body will, because his life in you is joined to your spirit, and you will live forever."

Sara knew this was a difficult thing for her sister to understand in a phone conversation, but she wanted her to have the assurance that she would live forever no matter what happened to her.

Death Knocks Twice

R-r-r-ring. Sara ran to the phone before it woke her mother, who was sleeping in the spare bedroom. Sara had just brought her home from the hospital where she had undergone a battery of medical tests. Her mother had a myriad of health issues, and Sara spent many days taking her to doctors.

"Aunt Sara, Mom has had another stroke, and this time there is no response. She's hooked up to life support, and the doctors say she's brain-dead. I thought you should know."

Sara hung up the phone and immediately went online to check flight availability to her sister's hometown. Then she called Nick, her neighbor, and her best friend to ask for help and alerted everyone to the fact that she had to leave town to go to her sister's bedside.

"I might not see her again," she told Nick as she said good-bye and walked into the passenger security area at the airport.

Nick nodded. His wife's relationship with her sister was short-lived.

"I'll be thinking and praying for you," he said, his heart heavy with compassion.

Sara relived her childhood memories of Jane during the plane flight, although they were few. There had been no closeness. What little existed had blossomed recently because of their discussions about God.

Sara exited the hospital elevator and proceeded to Jane's room in ICU. Callie stood outside, rapt in a discussion with a doctor, whom Sara assumed was Jane's.

"They want to pull the plug on the machines," said Callie as the doctor walked away. "He said it's my decision, since I'm her daughter and next of kin."

Sara didn't respond. It was difficult to know what to say at such a grievous time. She took Callie's hand and held it tightly, then she walked into Jane's room.

The respirator droned on, and Sara looked for her sister's face underneath the mass of tubes and wires. The monitor beeped and was filled with numbers and a jagged line that depicted Jane's heartbeat.

"She's still alive," Sara said to Callie.

"She's breathing, but she's not doing that on her own. The machine is breathing for her. The doctor says there is no brain activity and that she won't recover."

According to the medical personnel, Jane's prognosis was grim, and death was inevitable. But Sara believed in miracles and that Jesus could raise her from her deathbed.

She prayed silently. *Dear Jesus, please bring my sister back to life and heal her, but I trust you and ask you to do what is best for her. I place her in your capable hands. Please show me what you want me to do here.*

Sara could hardly find a spot to touch Jane's hand amid the needles and IV lines. The all too familiar smells of hospital rooms triggered a twinge in Sara's head.

"Please, God, don't let me get a migraine. I need to be here for my sister."

The pain subsided, and Sara sat in a chair beside the bed. "Please God, have mercy on my sister."

Callie had left the room, but this time, she entered with the announcement that the doctors wanted to take Jane off life support, and that anyone who might want to say goodbye should be notified so he or she could come to the hospital. People were notified that the time was short, and Jane would be gone soon.

The Machines Stop

The next morning, the elevator doors opened, and Jane's doctor and his nurse walked down the hallway and entered her room. Callie and Sara stood beside Jane's bed.

The doctor said, "I'm going to unplug the ventilator and the other equipment."

The whoosh, whoosh, whoosh of the ventilator stopped, and the technology ceased. The nurse took the mouthpiece and tube from Jane's mouth and removed all the tubes connected to the machine. The doctor told them that Jane would be gone within hours.

Three days after the machines were silenced, Jane was still breathing and alive.

"There's a reason she's still here," said one of Jane's attending nurses. "There must be some unfinished business."

Sara immediately thought of her conversation regarding forgiveness that she had had with Jane several years earlier while Jane lay in her hospital bed.

'He who curses his mother or his father will surely die.' Jane, you need to forgive your mother.

Oh, please, don't tell me that, she said. *That means I will never get well.*

This was the day, and Sara was witnessing the fulfillment of that Bible verse resulting from Jane's decision to ignore it.

That evening, as Sara prayed for her sister, she heard God speak to her in an almost audible voice.

"There's something you must do, Sara. You must take your sister through a process of forgiveness so she can release the people that she has never forgiven and be free," spoke the Lord God into Sara's spirit.

She knew she heard God's voice and that she must obey. However, she didn't know how she would do it or what would happen as a result. She called some friends she knew in the town and asked them to come to the hospital.

Within hours, Sara greeted her Christian friends and closed the door of Jane's hospital room, so they could all be alone. Jane's shallow breaths were the only sounds in the room.

The husband and wife team softly played the zither and sang praises to God. Their voices were angelic and beautiful.

The Cross of Christ

Sara bent over and placed her lips next to Jane's ear. She believed that her sister could hear every word, because the Holy Spirit within her was alive. She knew Jane's history and the number of people with whom she had broken relationships and genuine hatred in her heart. Jane's dealings with family members were well-known, even though she had not been in close proximity to Sara.

"Jane, I want you to picture the terrible, ugly rugged wooden cross that your Savior Jesus Christ died upon for your sins. Jesus is not on that cross anymore. He is standing in front of it, in his white flowing robes, with his hands outstretched towards you. I want you to take your mother by the hand and together stand before Jesus."

Sara took a deep breath. She trusted God that she was saying what he wanted her to say.

"Jane, hold your mother's hands and turn towards her. I want you to tell her how angry you've been. 'Mother, I have been filled with anger and hatred towards you for a very long time. I don't know when it started, but I ask you to forgive me for hating you. Please forgive me for all of the nasty things I have said and done to you.'"

"Now, Jane, I want you to turn to Jesus Christ and ask him to forgive you for hating your mother. Repeat after me. 'Please forgive me, Jesus, for my sin of anger and hatred towards my mother.' Then turn to your mother and release her into God's hands and set her free. 'Mother, I forgive you in the name of Jesus. I place you in his hands and set you free. I forgive you because Jesus Christ has forgiven me.'"

As her friends Paul and Amanda played, sang, and filled the room with music, Sara led Jane in prayers of forgiveness for her ex-husband, an aunt, her brothers, and herself, Sara. She repeated the same pattern of telling Jane to take each person by the hand

and stand before Jesus Christ, both asking for forgiveness and forgiving each individual.

The time was late, and Sara gathered her things to go back to her hotel. As she kissed Jane on the cheek, tears fell from Jane's eyes. The tortured grimace that had been on her face had changed to a sweet smile. She knew the doctor's diagnosis was that Jane was brain-dead, but Sara knew that something powerful had happened inside of Jane's soul.

The Visitors

"Oh, my. I can't believe this!" said Sara upon her arrival at the hospital the next morning. Both her mother and brother stood outside of Jane's hospital room. They had just arrived from the airport.

Her mother was visibly upset, confused and barely able to walk. Her son held her by the arm as he led her into Jane's room and helped her into the chair beside the hospital bed. Jane's mother took her hand and cried.

"Oh, Jane, I'm so sorry this has happened to you."

Sara could not hear the rest of what her mother said to Jane, but she knew that it was necessary for the meeting to take place.

Sara stood by in amazement as, one by one, each of the family members whom Jane had forgiven came to Jane's room and sat beside her bed. Inaudible words were spoken, tears were shed, and good-byes were said. By the end of the day, everyone had come and made peace with Jane. Jane's peace had been reached the night before.

By six o'clock in the evening, all had gone home, except for Sara and Callie. They kept a vigil beside Jane's bed and listened to Jane's guttural breathing.

Sara was sitting on the floor at the foot of Jane's bed. "There is a presence in this room," she said softly. She knew that Jesus Christ had come to take her sister home to her place in heaven.

The heavy, labored breathing stopped, and the room filled with an indescribable peace.

At two o'clock in the morning, death knocked the third time, and Jane answered. She was free to leave this earth, freed by forgiveness.

11

A New Career

"Dr. Campbell, you have helped me so much since I first came to you for counseling, both Nick and me. I would like to become the kind of counselor you are, leading people to know Jesus Christ and his forgiveness. Can you tell me where you received your training?"

"This type of counseling is called 'exchanged life' or 'grace-life,' and you can't learn it at the university. You must go to a counseling center where they will teach and train you to be able to help others. Do you believe that is what you want to do?"

"Absolutely! What we have done together in our sessions, and what I have learned have changed my life, and consequently that of my family. We are different people, both Nick and I. I want to be able to teach others how to allow God to change their lives, too. Nick wants me to pursue this."

Sara spent the next few years learning the skills necessary to teach others how to let God bring them freedom from their pasts. When she had finished her counseling internship, her first client arrived at her office. Her name was Andrea.

12

Andrea's Story—Ten Years Earlier

Andrea's mother ran toward her as Andrea and her boyfriend walked arm in arm down the sidewalk. "Your brother's dead! Oh my god, he's dead! Let's go! You need to come now!"

Grabbing Andrea's arm and pulling her away from Darren, she ran with her daughter toward the house. They got there as the paramedics were hoisting the stretcher into the ambulance. The black, ominous body bag concealed a lifeless son and brother, Josh.

"What happened?" Andrea screamed. "How could this have happened? Where was he? What was he doing? Let me see him."

Her mother, Jennifer, put her arm around her daughter's shoulders to restrain her. "No, they need to take him now. It's best if you don't see him. We found him hanging by a rope in the basement. Just go in the house and be with your father. He's in the living room."

The eighteen-year-old daughter excitedly ran up the steps to the front porch, pulled open the screen door, and saw her father sitting on the sofa. He raised his head from his hands as she approached.

"Dad, I don't understand. What happened? How could he do this—kill himself? I don't understand."

"I hadn't seen him for a few hours, and I went looking for him. When he didn't answer my calls, I looked all over the house and then went down into the basement. He must've climbed up on a chair and then kicked it out from under him. Why, God, why?" he said as he shook his head side to side.

Andrea sat beside her father on the tattered sofa with the garish print. The furniture was old and worn, telling stories of many years of neglect.

Buzz-z-z-z, rang the doorbell.

Andrea rose and through the screen door saw two policemen.

"Hello, miss. Are your parents home? We are Sergeants O'Rourke and Scarpino. We need to ask you some questions about your brother."

"Do you have to do this now?" Andrea said. "My dad is pretty upset, and I don't know where my mother is."

As she said that, Jennifer appeared behind the policemen.

"What do you want?" she said.

"Ma'am, I know this is a very difficult time, but we need to ask you some questions about your son."

"Can't you wait a little while? We are all reeling from finding him."

"Ma'am, we need to determine whether this was a suicide or some other cause of death."

"What do you mean, some other cause of death? We found him hanging from a rope in the basement. My poor Joshua, my poor, poor Joshua."

"Did he seem distraught to you?"

"He was very quiet. Had always been quiet, since he was a little boy. He stayed in his room a lot, playing games on the computer."

"Had there been any arguments in the family, anything that he was particularly upset about? How about school, his friends? Did he have problems at school or with any of his friends? How about girlfriends? We're just trying to find out what might have made him take his life."

"His father and I weren't home much, and his sister left home to go and live with her boyfriend." She looked at Andrea as she spoke. "I guess he was alone most of the time. He was really smart and did well in school, but as far as I know, he didn't have many friends. He was kind of, what do they call really smart kids today, kind of a nerd or a geek. He spent most of his time on the computer, at least that's where I'd find him when I came home from work."

"How old was your son, ma'am?"

"He just turned twelve. Look, Officer, I need to sit down. I feel like I'm going to faint."

"Of course," said Sergeant O'Rourke. "I'm so sorry we had to bother you. We'll be leaving now, and we'll call if we need to talk again."

As the rickety door closed behind the officers, Andrea's mother sank into the sofa beside her husband. Andrea was on his other side, and no one spoke.

As she got up from her seat, Andrea turned and stared at her parents. Shaking her head in disgust, she walked away slowly and left the house. She would not return.

On her way down the porch steps, she called her boyfriend Darren. "I'm on my way. This time, I've left home for good. I can't believe they did nothing to help him. He killed himself! They must've noticed something. Either that, or they were just too stupid or drunk to pay any attention to him. I never should've left him, but now I can't be in that horrible house. He died in the cellar, all alone. I can't stand even the thought of staying there."

"Come on back to the apartment," said Darren. "We'll go get something to eat, okay?"

"I can't eat," she said. "I feel like I'm going to throw up."

"Then we'll stay here. Whatever you want to do is fine. Just come home."

Andrea and Darren married within months, and Andrea left the city where she had been raised.

Out of Here

"When are you going to get a job?" she said as she watched Darren light up some weed. "I'm pretty sick of being the only one who's working."

"Why do I need to get a job? Between food stamps and my welfare check, we're doing all right."

"Well, that's not enough for me. I can't stand it that I go to work and you sit home, watch TV, and smoke pot all day. I'll give you a month to get a job, or I'm out of here."

"Are you threatening me?" said Darren. "I thought you were okay with this arrangement. I never promised you that I would get a job. I thought you just wanted to party, have fun, and get high with me."

"Well, maybe I did, but I don't now. I want things to change. I'm sick and tired of this."

One month later, Andrea stood at their bedroom door with divorce papers in hand.

"Here, sign these. I told you things had to change or I was out of here. I guess you didn't believe me. I'm done," she said.

The Promotion

I've never been in the manager's office before, Andrea thought. *I wonder what's up?*

"Andrea, your computer skills are pretty good, and I think you'd do well as a data processor. Does that interest you?"

"Yes, sir, it does."

Andrea had become more engaged in her job since she divorced Darren. It gave her a new focus.

Her manager stared at her, ogling her short skirt and form-fitting blouse.

"How about if we place your desk right outside my office? Then I can keep a sharp eye on you," Mr. Riley said as he lowered his voice.

"Andrea, would you go to lunch with me? I'd like to get your opinions on some things," he said six months later.

Andrea gloried in the attention he paid her.

"Of course. Lunch sounds great."

Lunches in the coffee shop around the corner from the office persisted until one day he said, "Andrea, my wife is away for a couple of weeks. Would you come to my apartment after work?"

The affair began that night and didn't conclude until a pregnancy was terminated by an abortion. Both Mr. Riley and Andrea agreed that she should move on to another job, one far away from him and his family. He referred her to a manager friend of his. She was twenty-one.

Same Song, Second Verse

The new position entailed her setting up hotels, meals, and entertainment for the managers when they were with their clients. Drinking was part of the picture, and Andrea was responsible for stocking the bar with whiskey and mixers. She learned that she could drink a good amount without appearing drunk. She drank—well.

"Andrea, could you stay late and clean up this mess?" her new manager said. He had the same air about him as Mr. Riley, and she didn't trust him.

"I really need to get home tonight," she said. "It's awfully late. Can't the cleaning crew take care of it?"

Before her words had fallen from her mouth, her boss pushed her onto the counter and pinned her arms above her head. His body pressed down on hers, and she couldn't scream.

"C'mon, Andrea, I know we can have a good time. Just relax and let it happen. Sam Riley told me all about you."

With muffled sobs, she didn't fight him. Afterwards, she took her belongings and left the hospitality suite.

Disheveled, she walked to her car. *He raped me. He raped me.* The words loomed in her mind. *How could I have been so stupid?*

She arrived at work the next morning before anyone else and cleaned out her desk. She wanted to escape before he appeared. Placing her letter of resignation on his desk, she left.

Drowning

"Can I buy you a drink?" the well-dressed man said. "Are you waiting for someone?" He sat down on a bar stool next to hers.

"Really, I want to be alone. You men are all alike, always trying to score."

"Is that what you think I'm doing? I noticed you were alone, and I thought you might like some company."

"Well, I don't, if it's okay with you."

He turned aside and ordered a drink. "Bartender, I'll have what she's having, and bring her another one."

"I told you I'm not interested in company, especially male company."

"What's got a burr under your saddle? Are you mad at all men, or just those who want to buy you a drink?"

"Look, buddy, will you just bug off? It's been a really bad couple of days."

"Can I help you in some way?"

"Right now, there's no help for me. I need a new job and a new life for that matter."

"I have a small company. Let me give you my card. Call me and I'll see if I could have something for you. What is your skill set?"

"I'm pretty good on the computer and in organizing things."

"Call me," he said as he slipped his card into her hand.

Andrea took it and noticed his kind eyes. She hadn't seen kindness in anyone for a long time.

"I can't find a job anywhere. I've put out a ton of resumes with not even one response. I'm scared I'll run out of money and not be able to afford to live here," Andrea said to her landlord.

Turning away from Mr. Smothers's door, her fingers brushed the card in her pocket.

"He said to call him. I guess I might have to," she muttered as she walked up the two flights to her apartment. "I just hope he's not like all the other guys I've met in this town."

"You've got the job," the man with the kind eyes said. "I can really use some help in this office. It's been just me for a while, but I think we're at the point that I can bring someone else on board. I need someone to enter everything into the computer, pay invoices, and keep track of everything. Do you think you can do that?"

Andrea felt the knots in her stomach. She was tempted to run, but she was desperate.

"I'm sure I can help you and get the job done," she said.

"Good. Can you start right now? Do you see this stack of bills on my desk? How about if we start with them?"

"Well, we set up the online banking and paid the bills. At least we got that all done today," she said as she slung her purse over her shoulder. "I'll see you in the morning."

"Whew," she breathed as she walked to her car. "I guess I passed that test."

One year later, Tony Scott stood before her desk. "Andrea, I'd like to give you a little one year anniversary gift," he said as he reached into his pocket and pulled out a black velvet box. Pushing up the lid, he said, "Will you marry me? I think we make a pretty good team, and we can work together and grow this company. What do you say?"

Stunned, she didn't speak for a few minutes. Collecting her thoughts, she said, "Tony, just because we work well together doesn't mean we should get married. We don't even love each other."

"Oh, but I do love you. I love you very much, and I want you to be my wife. This isn't just an impulsive gesture. I've been thinking about this for months. Will you at least think about it?"

"Okay, I promise to think about it."

I do trust him, and I respect him, too. He's smart and probably has a good future. I have seen worse. He's certainly a lot better than my first husband, that jerk Darren, she said to herself, as she walked to her car and clicked the remote. *He'll make a lot of money someday.*

Tony and Andrea married in a civil ceremony at the justice of the peace. The justice's staff were their witnesses, and no friends or family were invited.

"I wish I could've invited my parents," she said to Tony as they walked down the courthouse steps.

"We didn't need anyone else, Andrea. I just wanted you all to myself."

Andrea felt uneasy at that remark, but she ignored it.

The First Year

"Haven't you had enough to drink?" she said as they sat at the bar. "I'm tired and want to go home."

"Aww, just one more, honey. Loosen up a little bit. You're wound up too tight. I need to relax after a long day."

She sighed and let him order her another drink. *If you can't buck 'em, join 'em,* she thought.

The next morning, Andrea sauntered into the kitchen as Tony was pouring himself some black coffee.

"Want some?" he said.

"No, but I think I need some aspirin and something for a hangover. I didn't know you could drink so much. You drank me under the table, and I'm the one with the hangover."

"It helps me to relax. You're okay. You'll get used to it. We need to get to the office."

Every workday culminated in a stopover at the bar near their office, and the weekends gave opportunities for more drinking.

"Scotch and soda, jigger of gin," the old song blared over the sound system.

"Tony, I think you're turning into an alcoholic. Can we order dinner without the booze?"

"I don't have a problem. You're imagining things. I like to unwind. You can go on home if you want. I'll call you a cab."

"I don't want to leave you, but I'm afraid to ride in the car with you. I'll stay so I can drive. I'm not as high as you, and, besides, I'm pregnant."

The kind eyes suddenly changed to a glare of disapproval. "I thought we weren't having kids," he said.

"I know that's what we decided. I didn't plan this, but that's the way it is. I wish you could be a little more understanding. I'm not happy about it either, but I do want this baby. I've had one abortion, and I'm not having another. I think it will help things get better."

"There's nothing wrong that needs to get better. Hey, Jerry, can you get me another manhattan?" He turned his face away from hers and toward the bartender.

She sat on the barstool in silence and ordered a drink. *I wish this night would end*, she thought.

Baby Woes

"You'll have to bring her to work with you," Tony said. "I can't afford for you to stay home with her, and I certainly can't hire someone to take your place. The baby wasn't my idea, so you're going to have to figure out how to work and take care of her at the same time. You were supposed to be my Girl Friday, not a mother."

"That really hurts me, Tony. She is our baby, not just mine. I never thought I could love a baby like I love her, but I do. I wish you would look at her and love her, too."

"I'm not the father type. I didn't grow up with a father, and I don't want to learn to be one."

As Andrea looked into Tony's eyes, darkness drove out the light that she saw when they met.

"How can you expect me to bring Alice to the office, work, and take care of her at the same time? I need to nurse her, change her, bathe her. You're asking me to do something that's impossible!"

"You figure it out. I told you I never wanted kids in the first place. I wanted it to be you and me, that's all. There's no room in my life for a baby. I'm trying to build this company, and I thought that's what you wanted."

"I give up," she shouted, running into the bedroom. "I'm starting to hate you. Now, are you happy?"

Slam.

"That's the door. He didn't even hear me."

Andrea didn't go to work that day, and Tony didn't come home before she went to bed. The next morning she found him, clothes wrinkled and half off, sleeping on the sofa. She moved quietly around the apartment and left with Alice before he was awake.

R-r-r-r-ring. Andrea waited for someone to answer the phone.

"Hello," said her mother.

"Mom, I need to come home."

Andrea exited the cab with baby in tow. Her mother opened the door and ran toward her, all the while waving her arms in the air.

"A baby, you have a baby! Why didn't you let us know?"

"Because my husband, Tony, didn't want me to tell anyone, and we haven't spoken since Josh's death. Where's Dad?"

"He's in the house watching his shows. He's been laid off from his job, and now he sits at home doing nothing."

"Do you still have your job?" she said, handing Alice to her.

"Yes, but it is hard to pay for everything on my salary. It's been rough. Why didn't you ever call, or send us an e-mail, or something? We haven't known how to reach you."

"I didn't want to contact anyone after I left here. My desire was to put this house and what happened here as far behind me as possible. But, you know, I think about it every day, every day." Her voice trailed off.

They climbed the porch steps with the peeling paint and opened the same rickety wooden screen door.

Nothing's changed, Andrea thought. *Still as much of a mess as ever.*

Andrea walked from the bright sunlight of the summer's day into the living room with the drapes closed, the only light coming from the blaring TV.

"Joe, look who's here. And she's brought us a grandchild."

Josh's father barely removed his eyes from the screen. The game show had him mesmerized.

"He's like that every day. Sits in that chair watching one show after another. I swear, I think he'd starve to death if I didn't fix him some food."

Andrea quickly inspected the room visually. *Dark and bleak. But what's happened to him? This was a mistake, coming home. There's no home to come home to.*

Andrea's mother took the baby into the kitchen, all the while inquiring what she could do for her.

"Never mind, Mom," said Andrea. "I'll take care of her." *I'm not used to my mother helping me with anything*, she thought.

"So, tell me, why did you come? I suppose it's not just for a visit, since we haven't heard from you in years. You've left your husband, haven't you?"

"Yes, how did you know?" she said testily.

"Well, don't get mad, but you always did have a pattern of running away from things rather than facing them. I guess it's a family trait, now that I'm dealing with your father."

"I left home the first time because you and Dad drank every night after work, and I was sick of cleaning up after everyone. I'm sorry, but that's the way I felt. I didn't think it was my job to take care of my drunk parents. And then, after Josh's death, I couldn't handle it anymore. I can't believe you stayed in this house, with all those terrible memories. How could you live here after what happened in that basement?"

"Where was I going to go? We didn't have enough money to move, and then your father lost his job. We've been trapped in this house, and yes, with all those dreadful memories. Josh's death shook us to the core. So, why have you left your husband?"

"Because he's fast becoming an alcoholic, if he isn't one already. He thinks he's fine, but I grew up with two alcoholics, and I know all the signs. Now, with the baby, he doesn't want anything to do with her, and I feel like I'm on my own. I figured I might as well leave, but then I realized that I didn't have anywhere else to go."

"Well, your dad and I have stopped drinking. We joined a church and have been attending a twelve-step program, *Proclaim Recovery.* It's kind of like AA, but with a spiritual emphasis to it."

"Oh, no, don't tell me you've had a *Come to Jesus* experience. You've got to be kidding."

"No, I'm not, and it's not like that. Josh's death changed us, but we still have a long way to go. Your dad and I need a lot of help and a lot of healing. All I can say is we're trying, but it's not that easy. We haven't gotten to the eighth step yet, and when we do, I don't know if we'll be able to do it. It's about making amends and forgiveness. I just pray that I can let go of what's happened."

"Well, good luck with that. That's as far off my radar screen as it can get. I'm trying to get through today, let alone go back and worry about the past."

"That's just the point. I have learned that God sent Jesus to deal with my past. I don't have to do it on my own."

"I need to go take care of the baby," Andrea said, shutting down the conversation. She muttered, "One thing I don't want to hear about is religion."

Andrea heard her phone buzz with text messages. Looking down, she read them.

"Andrea, please come home. I'm sorry. I'll make it up to you, I promise. I need you."

"Yeah, right, he needs me. For what, his business? Well, I don't need him. *We* don't need him," she said, fixing her eyes on Alice.

Each day, Andrea ignored Tony's pleas on her phone. "I'm not answering him," she said to Jennifer as her mother passed by and commented on the buzzing phone.

"You can't ignore him forever," Jennifer said. "What do you think you're going to do, just serve him with divorce papers? This is your second marriage, right? Or was there another one along the way? Maybe the two of you can get some help and learn how to make your marriage work."

"Mom, you're a great one to talk. You haven't had such a great marriage, at least not that I can remember. Do you really think you're in a position to give me marital advice?"

"Your father and I never divorced, although I know we weren't happy for years. I'm just saying that there is help available, I'm sure, if you want it."

"Okay, okay. I'll think about it. I want Tony to be a father to our daughter, and not just a businessman. I can't live with an alcoholic. Now that I have a child, I won't do to her what Josh and I went through as kids."

"You keep bringing that up to me, and I'm sorry for that. I hope that you can forgive us someday for our drinking and neglect of you and your brother."

"Forgive you? What makes you think you deserve forgiveness?"

"That's just it, Andrea. I don't deserve it. No one does. But that's why Jesus came to this earth, to die for me so that I could be forgiven. He forgave me when he died on the cross for me, and only when you can accept that for yourself will you understand how you can be forgiven, and in turn forgive me and your father."

"Why do I have to be forgiven? You're the ones who drank, who didn't take care of us, and who left Joshua alone so he could take his life."

"Okay, Andrea. I won't argue with you. Please understand that I am very, very sorry for all my sins of the past. I have asked God for forgiveness, and he has forgiven me."

"It's that easy, right? All you have to do is say you're sorry and you're forgiven? You don't have to pay for what you've done?"

"I wish I could, but I can't. There's nothing I can do to pay for my sins, my drinking and neglect. God knew that. That's why Jesus had to die, because I could never do enough to pay for my sins. He had to die and take my sins into his body in order to forgive me."

"Enough. I'm done," said Andrea, getting up from the table and walking away.

Jennifer lowered her head and prayed. "Dear Lord, open her eyes to understand who you are and what you've done for her. Reveal her own sin to her and your love for her in the cross of Jesus."

Later that night, after her parents were asleep, Andrea descended into the basement—a place she had avoided since her return home. Standing on the cold concrete, flashbacks bombarded her mind.

Andrea, can I talk to you for a second? Joshua said.

Not now, geek, she said. *Can't you see I'm in the middle of something?*

Andrea, can you walk home from school with me? There's this kid who says he's going to beat me up after school.

Oh, you're just imagining things. You need to toughen up, Josh. Learn to fight if someone hits you.

Andrea, I need your help. Please help me. Please help me! Joshua screamed at her from a deep pit.

Andrea fell to her knees. "Oh, no, I was the one who ignored him. He needed me and I blew him off. I'm the guilty one. It was me. He needed my help," she cried as she prostrated herself on the floor.

Much later, she arose, blew her nose, wiped the tears from her face, and slowly walked up the stairs.

"Forgiveness. Forgiveness." She spoke the words repeatedly as she turned out her light.

Come to Jesus

"Where are you guys going?" Andrea greeted her parents as they sat at the kitchen table in their dressy clothes.

"To church," said her father. "Would you come with us?"

"No, thank you. You go without me. I'll stay here with Alice."

"They have a nursery there with wonderful sweet ladies who sit and rock the babies. Are you sure you wouldn't like to come?" Jennifer said.

"No, that's fine."

Alone in the empty house, the pictures of Joshua begging her for help flooded her mind as she sat and fed Alice. "Oh, no, God, please make this stop. I can't make this stop."

The voice was almost audible, but it sounded like it was coming from inside her head. *No, you can't make it stop. Only I can. Call out to Jesus. He's waiting for you to forgive you.*

Andrea looked around but saw no one. Her body was flushed with heat. After putting Alice in the pack 'n play, she cautiously entered the basement again. She stared at the place where Joshua died.

"Oh, my gosh. I see Jesus dying on the cross and looking at me. Jesus, are you real? Are you here?"

Falling to her knees, she cried out, "Jesus, please forgive me for my horrible sins against my brother. He needed me, and I was too selfish to pay any attention to him. Oh, Jesus, I'm sorry. I'm so sorry. There's nothing I can do to help him now. He's gone, and it's my fault. Lord, help me, please. I've been so wrong, so angry and selfish. Forgive me."

"Andrea, where are you? I'm going to make us some lunch. Andrea, Andrea?"

Andrea, lying face down on the cold concrete, heard her mother's footsteps moving through the house. Then the door to the basement opened.

"Andrea, are you down there? What are you doing?"

Jennifer walked slowly down the steps.

"Oh, my gosh, are you all right?"

"Yes, I'm okay," Andrea said as she arose, wiping her face on her pajama sleeve.

"Did you fall? What happened?"

"I don't know. I can't talk about it right now. I just want to go lie down."

As she stood up, she felt different but didn't know why.

The Visitor

The next Sunday, Andrea asked her parents if she could accompany them to church.

"Sure," said Jennifer.

"I'm just going to sit here in the back with the baby," Andrea said, "if that's okay with you. I might not stay."

Jennifer and Joe walked further down the aisle and took their seats.

"Why aren't we sitting with Andrea and Alice?" said Joe to his wife.

"I think she wants to be by herself. It's a miracle that she's here at all. You know Andrea, you can't push her or pressure her. Let's just pray for her."

Andrea continued to visit the church with her parents, until one day she mustered the courage to approach the pastor.

"I liked your sermon," she said. "I guess forgiveness is an important thing to learn about. I'm Andrea, and I'm visiting my parents," she said as Alice squirmed in her arms.

"Good to meet you. Yes, forgiveness is very important. You can come and talk to me about it if you'd like."

"No, that's all right. I think for now I'll just visit."

Returning

"I've decided to go home and try and make my marriage work. I don't want to raise Alice without a father," Andrea said to her parents a month later.

"I think that's wise," said Jennifer. "If we can help you in any way, please call. Let's not stay apart like we did after Joshua's death. I know you have a lot going on, but I want you to know that I'm here for you."

"Thanks, Mom. I'll try to remember that. Maybe I can find a church for us when I get back home."

"I'm so glad to see you," her husband said. "Please don't ever leave me again. I didn't know what to do without you. I thought I was going crazy, and I want you to know that I tried to stop drinking for you, but I haven't been able to shake the habit of drinking after work."

"Maybe we need some help with our problems. Would you be willing to try?"

"What does that mean, 'help?'"

"I don't know, but when I was away, I started going to church. My parents have stopped drinking, and they're going through some program called *Proclaim Recovery.* It doesn't have to be that, but I think we could find someone to help us figure out what's wrong."

"Wow. They've quit. I know you never thought that would happen. Something really big must've happened to cause that."

"I think it was my brother's death that woke them up, although my dad seems very withdrawn now. I'm sure they have a long way to go, but at least they're trying. I never thought Josh's death affected me so much, but down deep in my gut, I know it did. I don't know what to do with it all, but I want to get past it. I've never put much stock in looking back at the past, but now I do. I have Alice to think about now, and I don't want to put a lot of bad stuff onto her."

"I don't want a divorce," he said, "so if you think getting help could change things and help me at least to cut down on my drinking, then I'm willing to try."

"Do you think you could rethink your role as Alice's father, too?"

"That's a tough one, because you know that I never wanted kids."

"I know, but she's here now, and we can't send her back. She's our responsibility, and I don't want her raised in an alcoholic home like I was. Things have to be different. They just have to get better. If it's alright with you, I'm going to look for a church that has the *Proclaim Recovery* program. My parents are going, and it's helping them."

The Light Comes On

The next Sunday, Pastor Jim promoted the beginning of the new season of *Proclaim Recovery.* Andrea felt like he was talking right to her as she listened to his sermon. Her husband seemed a bit uncomfortable in his seat, but he listened, too. Andrea filled out a registration card for the class and handed it in after church.

"For the first time in a while, I feel hopeful," she said.

Tony looked away, and she knew he was thinking about what she said.

"Look, Tony, I know you're not sure about all this, but if we want this marriage to make it, I believe we need to go to this class together."

"Okay," he said, "I guess I'll give it a try. It can't hurt me, can it?"

13

Proclaim Recovery

"Let's go, Tony. I don't want to be late to the first class."

"All right, but I'm not sure about this."

"Aw, c'mon, let's try it. We won't go back if we don't like it."

"Oh, my gosh. That's someone from my high school days," said Andrea. "I wonder what she's doing here."

"Hi," said Lisa. "Remember me? From high school? I haven't seen you for years. Is this your first time here?"

"Yeah," Andrea said. "Have you been here before? I don't know where to go."

"I'm a group leader, and I'll show you around. Let me take you in and introduce you to your leader."

"Wow, this is a big place," said Andrea. "It looks like a living room."

"Andrea, this is Rachel," Lisa said. "I'll let you two get acquainted, and I'll take your husband to the men's groups. Don't worry. I'm sorry I didn't introduce myself to you. I didn't get your name," she said as she stretched her hand out toward Tony.

"Tony," he said, reaching out his hand.

"There are men's and women's groups so they can be free to talk without their mates or significant others. There are a lot of singles, divorced, and married in our groups, so you'll be sure to fit with someone."

"Okay, thanks," said Tony.

The leader of the program stood and explained the purpose of *Proclaim Recovery*—to bring freedom through a relationship with Christ and then to bring freedom into your relationships.

"Introduce yourselves to the group and tell a little about yourselves," said Tony's group leader.

"I'm Tony, and I'm here because my wife brought me."

A few of the men smiled, and one snickered. Some had been in *Proclaim Recovery* in the last session and were going through it again.

"I came the first time with my wife," said Larry, "but now I'm here for me. I can't get free from drugs by myself. I've tried. I need help."

"How was it?" said Andrea, meeting Tony at the glass doors.

"It was okay, but I'm not sure it's for me. People sitting around talking about themselves. That's not what I want to do."

"Why don't you try it one more time?" said Andrea. "It's hard to judge something in one visit."

"You might be right," he said. "I can't believe all these leaders do this for nothing, that they don't get paid for leading these groups."

"Not everything involves money," said Andrea. "Wouldn't it be nice to do things for others just because you want to? I know I've never known people like that, but I'd like to be one. I'm ready for a change."

"Boy, I don't know if I know you anymore. You sure are different."

"Really? I hope that's a good thing."

"Maybe, maybe not. I'll have to think about it."

The Eighth Step

"I don't know if I can do this," said Andrea, listening to the Recovery leader talk about making restitution. "Why should I forgive? Doesn't that just say that what people did to me was okay? Oh, my gosh, he must've heard me, because he just said that forgiving someone doesn't mean that what they did to you was right or excused. It is a communication and resolution between you and God."

She opened her notebook and prayed a prayer that was written on the assignment sheet. "Search me, O God, and know my heart! Try me and know my thoughts! And see if there be any grievous way in me, and lead me in the way everlasting!" (Ps. 139:23–24).

"I guess I'll just go with it and see what happens. Help me, God."

She started to write, and by the end of the hour, she had a list of names. The first ones were her mother and father.

"Your assignment is to go home and write a letter to each person on your list. Ask for forgiveness for each thing you've done to wrong him, or offer forgiveness to him for what he's done to wrong you," her leader said.

"But what if I can't see that person to talk to him?" said Andrea. "Like some of my bosses."

"Your letters are between you and God first. If you can't talk to the person, you still write them. It's either to offer him forgiveness or ask for it personally."

"I don't know if I can do this," she said, closing her notebook.

"How was it?" Tony said later that night.

"It was hard. About forgiveness. Some things I've never thought about."

"Are you upset?" he said. "You don't have to go to that thing, you know."

"No, I want to go," she said. "I wish you would go with me. I don't know why you quit."

"It wasn't for me, but you can go if you want."

"How's the baby?" she said, changing the subject.

"Okay. She went right to sleep. I think she's getting used to me."

Andrea smiled and turned away, carrying her class notebook into the bedroom.

"You're a million miles away," said Tony. "I've been talking to you, and I don't think you've heard a word I've said."

"I have a lot on my mind," she said as she wiped Alice's face with a baby wipe at breakfast. "We need to get going."

But They're the Ones Who Were Wrong

"*Proclaim Recovery* is tomorrow night, and I haven't done any of the assignment. I need some time by myself," she said, getting up from the dinner table.

"Okay, I'll put Alice to bed. I'm starting to like doing that."

Andrea readied for bed and climbed up onto the four poster with her notebook. Opening it, she stared at the names. "Dad, Mom, Joshua, Mr. Noble, Darren, Tony. I'm mad at a lot of people."

She wrote haltingly.

> *Dear Mom. I've wanted to talk to you about this stuff for years, but I never had the guts. Why did you leave me home all those times to take care of Joshua? Why did you come home drunk and not ask how we were or what we needed? Nothing was important to you except your booze, and we knew it. You would kick off your shoes, throw yourself onto your bed, and we wouldn't see you until the next morning. You didn't make us anything to eat. It was my job. Why did you have us if you didn't want to take care of us?*

Wiping her tears off the page with a Kleenex, she continued.

I pretty much raised myself, and Joshua. I know he missed you, and he must've suffered a lot because you weren't here. I didn't know how much it affected him, and me, but it did. I knew we were 'latchkey kids,' and I thought that was good because I was responsible. But if you want to know how I felt every day coming home by myself to an empty house, I felt abandoned. I would wait for you to come home, and then you'd come home drunk and fall asleep. And Joshua? Joshua was a lot younger than me. I'm sure he didn't feel like you cared at all. He pretty much never saw you. I was too young to be a mom to him, and I ran away from it and left home.

Mom, I hate you. I hate you for becoming an alcoholic and not taking care of us. We weren't important to you, not as important as your drinking. And I hate you for Josh's death. If you had been a mom, it never would've happened. You could've, should've stopped him. Why weren't you home when he died? Why did he have to die alone in the basement?

I feel drained, as if every bit of energy has been taken from me. I can't believe how much I have hated my mother. No wonder I don't get along with her.

Mom, forgive me for my part in our broken relationship. I know I am responsible for a lot of the fights we had, and my leaving home after Josh's death was a selfish thing to do. I haven't treated you like my mother for a long time, and I'm sorry. I have been angry and filled with hatred, and I need you to forgive me.

"Wow, this is really hard. I have so many more names on my list. The next one is my dad. This is a tough one."

Dad, I don't know why you drank. Was it so you and mom could be on the same page, or did you need to anesthetize yourself? I wanted to be your little girl all my life, and your drinking was more important than me. I would wait for you to come home, and some nights you stumbled in and fell asleep right away. Maybe it was to avoid arguing with Mom, I don't know, but I needed someone to be there for me. You failed me, big time. My friends would tell me about the things their fathers did with them, and I didn't have any fun stories. There were no stories. Mine would've been sad, if I had told anyone. Oh, this is so yucky. I can't find anything good to say about you. Maybe the fact that you're still here is the only nice thing I can say, but I'm not even sure about that. Why did you drink? You enabled Mom to keep drinking. You're a weakling, and you never stood up to Mom. You let her walk all over you, and I couldn't stand it. I wanted you to be a man, a father, and that didn't happen. You ignored Joshua because he wasn't like you. He wasn't interested in sports, wasn't a jock, and didn't yell at the television when you watched your football games. He liked science, math, the computer, and video games. He was your son, but you weren't a dad to him either. You didn't know either one of us, and I resent you for it. I hated our home, and it's your fault.

"This is hard work, and I'm getting angry thinking about all this." Andrea closed her notebook and fell asleep.

The next night, Andrea left work early to get to *Proclaim Recovery*. She hadn't finished her assignment and hoped she could work on it before her group began.

Rachel, her group leader, said, "So, how'd you do with your letters? Were you able to get any finished?"

"It was really hard. I finished one but couldn't finish the second one. I was exhausted."

"It is a hard thing to do, probably the most difficult thing in this whole program. Writing those letters doesn't come naturally, especially when we've held in a lot of stuff for a lot of years. But it can be very cleansing when we get to the point of forgiving others. That's the goal."

"I'm not there yet. I still don't understand why I have to keep asking for forgiveness when I was the one who had bad things done to me."

"I understand," said Rachel. "I'm not saying that the things done to you were okay, but you need to get rid of the anger and unforgiveness that have built up in your heart as a result of those things. That's what's hurting you, others, and your relationship with God. It creates a wall that has to come down. God is the only one who can give you the strength and ability to forgive. You can't do it yourself. May I see what you've done?"

Andrea opened her notebook and removed the letters to her parents. "I did okay on the one to my mom, but I couldn't finish writing to my dad."

"Dads are sometimes the hardest, especially for little girls, because we all want to be princesses in their eyes. We want to be special, and when that's missing, there's a big hole in our hearts. The most important relationship for a little girl as she grows is the one with her father. I think God set it up that way. It's to teach us about the love of our Father God. I'm sorry you didn't have that. A lot of us have missed that in our lives. Fathers can be difficult to forgive, but God is there to take you through the process," said Rachel.

"I am angry that I didn't have a normal childhood like my friends and didn't grow up with parents who took care of me. I can't get past it."

"Let me give you the name of a Christian Counselor. Her name is Sara, and she has seen many people going through *Proclaim Recovery*. She comes highly recommended. Why don't you call her?" said Rachel, handing a business card to Andrea.

"Do you think I need this?" said Andrea.

"If your goal is freedom from anger and unforgiveness, I believe she can take you to the next level, if you're willing to go there."

"I want to look at my parents without hating them," said Andrea.

"I haven't gone to Sara for counseling, but I do know many whom she's helped. I think her initial consultation is free, so you can go and see if you are comfortable with her. See what she has to say."

"I'll talk to Tony. Maybe he'll go with me."

"Don't push him. He has to make that decision for himself. I know he stopped coming here. How is he?"

"He's more involved with the baby, and that gives me the time to come here. He's babysitting tonight."

"That's good, a baby step for him. Be patient. God is working in your situation," said Rachel. "He's always working. We don't always recognize it."

"Okay, but being patient is the hardest thing for me."

"It took you twenty some years to get this way, and God needs to do things in his timing, his way," said Rachel.

"I'll call this counselor in the morning," said Andrea.

"Rock-a-bye-baby, on the treetop," Tony sang as Andrea walked through the kitchen door. "When the wind blows, the cradle will rock."

Andrea opened the nursery room door and saw Tony leaning over Alice's crib. "When the bough breaks," he sang.

"That's really sweet," she said, as Tony turned his head quickly.

"Shhh," he said, putting his finger to his lips. "She's almost asleep."

"Anything to eat in the fridge?" she said, as they walked out of Alice's room.

"There's some leftover pizza. I ordered out."

"Did she give you any trouble?" said Andrea.

"No. She's so good. I think we did okay together."

Two Weeks Later

Sara opened her office door and beckoned to Andrea, "Andrea? Come in."

Andrea laid the magazine on the table, grabbed her purse and jacket, and hurried across the waiting room. She noted the family pictures on the counselor's desk and the diplomas on the wall.

"Are you married?" she said to Sara as she turned and found the loveseat cushion behind her.

"Yes, but let's talk about why you're here today," Sara said, sliding into her desk chair seat.

Outside the snowflakes clung to the office window, but inside was welcoming and homey.

"My group leader at church suggested I might need to see you. Christian stuff is new to me, and there's a lot I don't understand."

"Andrea, let me tell you about what kind of counseling this is," said Sara. "It is not just Christian; it is Christ-centered, meaning Christ is the one we rely upon to do his work in your life. He knows you and your struggles, and he is ready to help you. My role is to take you through a process which will bring you to know, trust, and hear him. As we take this journey, I'll give you assignments and some books to read that will help you to grow in your faith in God. God will do the necessary work in you, and he will use me to guide and teach you."

"But I just want to learn to forgive. I'm not interested in a *journey*," said Andrea. "I don't understand what that will mean."

"That's okay. If you're a Christian and have accepted and trusted Jesus Christ to forgive your sins and be your Lord and Savior, then you're already on a journey. You just haven't realized it."

"I have asked Jesus to forgive my sins, and I've been attending *Proclaim Recovery*. I'm on the eighth step, and I'm angry at a lot of people, probably most of the people in my life. I'm supposed to write letters to them, but I don't see how that will solve anything. It's brought up a lot of things that happened in my past, and the more I think about them, the madder I get, especially at my parents. I don't see how forgiving them can change anything," said Andrea.

Sara said, looking into Andrea's eyes, "The one God is looking at now is you and what's hidden in your heart. When you hold anger and hatred against another, it not only affects your walk with God, but it influences every relationship in your life. It's similar to having a bottle of poison inside you that keeps spilling over to others. The poison embitters you, harms you, and harms others. It will turn you into a bitter woman, unhappy and critical of the world. Relationships cannot be healthy as long as you hold hatred in your heart."

"Wow," said Andrea. "That's a lot to think about. Why should I forgive them? They're the ones who did bad things. Why do they deserve to have me forgive them?"

"No one deserves forgiveness, Andrea. You and I don't, and the people in your life don't. I have a book I'd like you to read called *Freedom in Forgiveness*. I'd like you to read it before your next appointment and pay special attention to the chapter on bitterness. I believe it is chapter ten."

"Okay, I will," said Andrea.

Walking into their apartment, Andrea saw Tony lift Alice from her high chair and walk toward her crib. Dinner was underway on the stove, and she realized that Tony had prepared food for them.

"Where have you been?" he said. "I've been waiting hours for you."

"I told you I had a counseling appointment when I left work. Can't you handle things by yourself for a change?"

"I didn't say it for that reason," Tony said. "I was worried about you."

"Boy, that's a new twist. I didn't think you ever worried about me."

"Why would you say that? Of course, I worry about you, especially when you don't come home."

"You weren't too worried when I went to stay with my parents. You only wanted me to come home so I could work and make you money."

"Make me money? It's a business for us, not me," said Tony. "Where did that statement come from?"

"I just feel so angry tonight," Andrea said. "Thinking about my past and what others have done to me have brought up a lot of unresolved issues. Nothing is right, and I'm pretty unhappy."

She watched Tony walk out of the room and knew she had touched a nerve. He hadn't made her happy for a long time, perhaps never, and she was convinced he felt the same.

"Are we going to fight again?" she said. "Or, should we not talk to each other at all?"

"Whatever," he called from the next room. "Nothing I say will matter anyway."

"Fine," she said, slamming the bedroom door and kicking her shoes across the room. Most of their nights together ended this way with them in separate rooms.

"Wa-a-a-ah," Alice cried from her crib.

"See, you woke her up," Tony yelled.

Andrea chose to ignore him and waited for Alice's cries to stop. Climbing onto their bed, she lay her head on the pillow and said aloud, "God, what am I doing? What's the matter with me? I'm so angry I could scream at the top of my lungs. I need your help. I'm destroying everything. Can you help me?"

She watched the ceiling fan blades move clockwise, and as she quieted her insides, she heard an almost audible voice.

"Yes, I'll help you, but you have to let me."

Andrea knew she had heard God's voice. It both comforted and scared her. She reached into her purse, pulled out the book Sara had given her, and opened to the first page.

It's Time

"Come in, Andrea," said Sara, opening her office door. "What kind of week have you had?"

"Not too great," Andrea said. "My husband and I fought a lot. That's getting old, and we're both pretty sick of it."

"Do you remember at our last appointment I told you when you harbor anger in your heart, it affects every relationship? That could be the reason for the fighting. What did you learn from reading your assignment?"

"I learned a lot. The forgiveness book was written for me, especially the chapter on bitterness. I'm angry at most people in my life, and it's turned into bitterness. That's pretty much it, but what do I do about it?"

"You will have to forgive all those people and release the venom you have inside you towards them. It won't be easy, but God will give you what you need. I told you we're on a journey, and forgiveness is a necessary part of that journey."

"I think I heard God's voice telling me to let him help me."

"Really? That's awesome," said Sara. "Tell me, how did you hear his voice?"

"Tony and I had a fight, and I was very upset. I told God I was sick of ruining everything and being angry, and I asked him to help me. As I lay there, I heard a voice say that I had to let him help me, and I knew it was God. I don't know how to let him," said Andrea.

"That's why I'm here, to help you, to be the vessel God uses to teach you things about God, yourself, and forgiveness," said Sara.

Sara rose from her desk chair and wrote on the whiteboard: Galatians 2:20: "My old self has been crucified with Christ. It is no longer I who live, but Christ lives in me. So I live in this earthly body by trusting in the Son of God, who loved me and gave himself for me" (New Living Translation).

She continued, "When Jesus died on the cross over two thousand years ago, you died in him. You didn't die physically, because you're here, but who you were from the time you were born until you accepted Christ died in him, all your sin, your old self."

"But how could that have happened? I wasn't born yet," said Andrea.

"Jesus has always existed. He is eternal and has no beginning and no end. Genesis 1:1 tells us, 'In the beginning, God created the heavens and the earth.' At the beginning of creation, God already existed. He was there the day you placed your faith in Jesus Christ, but he chose you to be in him before he created the world. It says that in Ephesians 1:4b, 'even as he chose us in him before the foundation of the world, that we should be holy and blameless before him.' He placed you in him before creation, and you were in Christ when he died, was buried, and came out of the tomb. He died, and you died in him. The old angry, depressed Andrea is dead. You just have to believe that truth and act upon it."

"What would that mean, for my old self to be dead?" said Andrea.

"When a person dies, what happens? He gives up his life, his dreams, expectations of others, and literally control of everything.

When you died with Jesus, you died to the right to be angry and vindictive, and to expect anyone to say he's sorry. You died to your expectations of others and control of your life and others' lives. That all went into the tomb with Jesus. When he came out of that tomb and rose from the dead, you came out, too, a new person in Christ. I know that's a lot to process, but the scriptures say it has already happened. Your job now is to live your life trusting him. He is in you by the presence of his Holy Spirit, who is the life of Christ, and he can live his life through you, instead of your trying to solve your problems yourself. He can give you what you need, instead of your calling out to him for help when you crash."

Andrea said, "If I'm dead, then how can I forgive?"

"Jesus's life in you is forgiving. He died on the cross to forgive you, and with his power, his life in you, you have the ability to forgive, because he will forgive through you. I know this is all new to you, but I want you to think about the old Andrea and who she was. Draw a cross on a piece of paper, place Jesus on it, and you there with him. Write down what died with him when you died. That's your assignment for next week," said Sara. "Let's pray. Lord Jesus, open Andrea's heart and mind by your Spirit to understand her co-crucifixion with you and what that means for her life. Give her your grace to believe she died with you, but more importantly that she rose with you and is a new creation. The old has passed away, and the new has come. She is a new person. Please give her faith to believe that what your Word says about her is true." Sara raised her head and gave Andrea a sheet of paper with scriptures written on it. "Look up these scriptures and ask God to make them real. That's it, and I'll see you next week with your cross picture completed."

As Andrea walked to her car, the picture of Jesus on the cross and her there with him stayed on her mind. *God, make it real in my everyday life, please. Help me believe all this is true for me.*

Andrea unlocked the door, opened it, and was surprised. "This looks beautiful! How did you do all this?" she said to Tony.

"I wanted to make you something special. It's our anniversary, you know," Tony said.

"I'm so sorry. I forgot. I've been so wrapped up in my own stuff that I don't know what day it is, let alone the date," said Andrea.

"That's okay. C'mon, I thought maybe we could have a nice dinner and watch a movie or something."

Andrea was speechless. Tony hadn't been this nice to her since before they were married. "Have you done something terrible and are trying to make up for it? I don't understand all this."

"Just like you to get suspicious. Can't I do something nice without your thinking I have ulterior motives?"

Andrea remembered Sara's words. *You are a new person. The old you is dead.*

"Yes, of course, and I'm sorry. I wasn't expecting this, but it's really nice. I'm sorry I have nothing for you for our anniversary, but I didn't think we had a lot to celebrate."

"Can you meet me halfway?" Tony said. "I'm trying here."

You are a new creation. Sara's words echoed in her mind.

"I'll try, too, and I'll ask God to help us, okay?"

Tony was silent for a minute, but then said, "That would be good. I'd like that. I haven't said anything, but I've asked God to change me and help me be a better husband and father. I think something is happening inside me that I don't quite understand. I haven't wanted a drink for at least a couple of weeks."

Andrea wiped tears from her cheeks. They came uncontrollably as she digested Tony's words.

"Let's sit down and eat," Tony said.

Andrea inhaled the garlic smell of the Italian bread and spaghetti and meatballs, her favorite meal. Tony grabbed her hand across the table. It was a day of new beginnings.

14

Set Free

Andrea arrived early for her appointment with her counselor, Sara. As Sara beckoned her to sit down, she said, "How are you today, Andrea?"

"Nervous and a little excited."

"Good," said Sara. "I believe God wants to do something special today."

"I'm ready," said Andrea.

"Can you show me your picture of the cross that I asked you to do?" said Sara.

Her stomach quivering and hands shaking, Andrea opened her notebook and removed the picture. "I couldn't believe all the things I thought about as I did this. The old Andrea didn't love people, not my family, no one. I see her as a selfish girl, concerned only about herself. I was responsible for my brother's death, his suicide, and I may never forgive myself."

"Can you tell me about your brother? Joshua, right?"

"Right. He was a good kid, mostly kept to himself," said Andrea.

"Why do you blame yourself for his death?" said Sara.

"Because he asked me for help, and I ignored him. As I look back on it, I wanted him to get tough, to take care of the bullies

146

himself. He was very smart, and the kids teased him. He wasn't a jock, and he didn't fit with the cool kids, so he got beat up a lot."

"How did you treat him?" said Sara.

"Pretty badly," said Andrea. "I had a boyfriend, and he was my focus. I pretty much ignored my little brother."

"What about your parents?" said Sara.

"They were both alcoholics and drank almost every night. Joshua stayed in his room or the basement. They didn't take care of either of us. I've always blamed them for his suicide, but I know I could've helped him and stuck up for him. I think he must've been pretty scared of other kids. I should've talked to him, but I didn't. I feel so guilty." Andrea bowed her head and cried.

Sara grabbed a Kleenex from the box on her desk, and Andrea blew her nose. "We're all responsible for his death, and now that I know about heaven and hell, I'm not sure he's in heaven. That haunts me. I can't stop thinking about him. He could be in hell for killing himself," said Andrea.

Sara interrupted Andrea, "Andrea, only God knows where Joshua is, and he knew how he was suffering. Joshua is gone, but you will need to release him to God and let him be in control of what happened to your brother. It's not God's will for anyone to take his own life, but God understands everything, which you may never know."

"I think about him every day, and I wonder about the day he died. I wasn't home. If I had been, would it have been different? Could I have saved him?"

"But you didn't, and you have to give that all to God."

"How?"

"I'll help you. I'll leave you alone for a while to give you time to write a letter to Joshua. Do you think you can do that?" said Sara.

"Yes, but why?" said Andrea. "He's gone."

"It's a way for you to get out of your heart and mind all the things you carry about your brother and his death." Sara handed Andrea the box of Kleenex. "Here, you might need these."

Andrea opened her notebook, took her pen, and held it over the first line. "Oh, God, he was such a scrawny little kid, and I didn't know him, not the way a sister should know a brother. I need you, God. Why did Joshua have to die?"

Sobbing, she watched the tears blur the blue notebook lines. "I had no idea I was so upset about him."

Andrea forced herself to start the letter.

> *Dear Joshua, Why? Why? Why didn't you tell anyone what you were planning? Someone could've helped you. I know I was a selfish teenager who wasn't paying attention to your pain, and I'm sorry. Was suicide your only option? I guess without Mom, Dad, or me paying attention to you, you felt you had nowhere to go. You'll never know how bad I feel for what happened to you. I'm going to counseling, and I've learned that depression comes from internalizing anger. I was depressed most of my life, and you were, too, or you wouldn't have done what you did. You had a right to be angry about our family and the way kids treated you. But, you know what, Joshua? I'm angry, too. I'm angry at you for hanging yourself in the basement. I can't go home, and Mom and Dad have to live in that house with memories of your death. How could you do that to us? I'm angry at you, Joshua, so angry.*

Andrea took a deep breath, shocked at her words to her brother. She weakly stood up, turned the doorknob of the counseling office, and called out to Sara. "I'm finished," she said.

"Great," said Sara, walking toward her.

Andrea handed Sara the letter, and she perused it. "Are you ready to let go of Joshua?"

"I think so," she said.

"Andrea, you were not in control of Joshua's life or responsible for his death. Joshua made that choice, and although it's a horrific event in your life, you have to let God have it, or it will destroy you. You say you've been depressed most of your life. Holding anger towards your brother will keep you in depression and rob you of the joy God has for you."

Andrea took the letter from Sara's hand. "What do I need to do? I want to let him go. I think he's lived in my head since that terrible day, and it's driven me crazy."

"Picture Joshua sitting on the couch next to you. Read him the letter you've written. Then I will help you."

Andrea began to read. Her voice shook, and tears flowed. When she finished the last line, Sara said, "Now, I want you to take Joshua's hand and stand before the cross of Jesus Christ, the cross he died on to forgive you and Joshua for your sins. Jesus is standing in front of the cross, his hands outstretched to you, his white robes glowing. Ask Jesus to forgive you for ignoring Joshua and not being the big sister God would've wanted you to be. Then ask Jesus to forgive you for the anger and hatred you've harbored towards Joshua."

"Okay, but will you help me?"

"Yes, don't worry. Jesus is in you to take you through this. He forgave you when he died for you, but you need to release this to him to be free from it," said Sara.

"Jesus, forgive me for ignoring my brother and not caring about what he was going through. Forgive me for being selfish and only concerned about me. I've been angry at Joshua for years, and he was twelve when he killed himself. When I think of him, I feel angry. I want to give you all my anger towards my brother. I think I've hated him for doing this. Jesus, his death isn't about me, and I made it all about me. I'm so sorry."

Sara said, "Now, Andrea, you need to tell the Lord that you give up control of Joshua's death and whom you've blamed, yourself and your parents. You have no right to blame anyone. Only God is the judge, and that's not your job."

"Okay," said Andrea. "Jesus, I give up control of Joshua's death. I give up blaming myself, my parents, and finally Joshua. Forgive me for acting as their judge."

"Now, Andrea, I want you to turn to Joshua and tell him you forgive him for taking his life," said Sara.

"Josh, I forgive you for killing yourself," said Andrea.

"Now, reach down, open the door to the prison you've held him in, and release him into the hands of Jesus. Picture Joshua inside that prison and tell him you're setting him free and giving him to Christ," said Sara.

"Josh, I open the prison door and set you free. I give you to Jesus. I'm not responsible for you anymore. Jesus, take him from me, please," begged Andrea.

Jesus walked to the prison door, grasped Joshua's hand, and walked toward the heavens with him.

"Whew, that was so real. I saw Jesus take Joshua and walk away with him. Jesus had his arm around Josh's shoulder and was holding him close," said Andrea. "Did that really happen?"

"I know the presence of Christ is here, and I believe Jesus gave you that vision to hold onto. He is the one who did it, not me, so when you get to heaven, you can ask him about it."

"I want to go home and take a nap," said Andrea. "I could go right to sleep."

"Make sure you get home first." Sara laughed. "I don't want you to fall asleep in your car."

Sara saw Andrea in the ensuing weeks, and they worked through her list of those who had hurt her. Her marriage became solid, and she enjoyed a relationship with her parents built upon their relationship with Jesus and his forgiveness of them all.

Epilogue

Sara spent the next thirty years working with women who had been through traumatic circumstances in their lives. Women who had been sexually abused became her specialty, since she had learned to work through that event for herself and emerge victorious, forgiven and forgiving. She knew God had shown her a way to forgive that set her free, and she was to teach what she knew to others. Through God's power, Sara was able to see many women freed by forgiveness and the giving of themselves and their pasts to Jesus Christ. As a result, women were saved as well as their marriages and families. Her husband Nick and twins Madison and Michael benefitted from the grace she received from God, and they also looked to Jesus to lead them into their futures. They are a strong, faith-filled family, and they are thankful to God for all he has done.

Appendix A

Chapter Questions

Prologue

1. What reason does Nick give for leaving Sara?

2. What is the present state of their marriage? What is their history?

3. What suggestion does Emma make to Sara?

4. What kind of help did Emma have with her marriage? Describe her first year of marriage.

Chapter 1

1. Describe Sara's neighbor, Alan.

2. Describe Sara's family and her relationships within her family.

3. Describe Alan's family. What could be wrong with David?

4. Why did Sara lose her relationship with Alan?

5. What was the Mathesons' response to David's sin against Sara? Who was punished for it?

6. What results of the abuse did Sara carry with her?

Chapter 2

1. Describe Nick's home situation.

2. Who are the men in Nick's life?

3. Why is Nick's mouth washed out with soap, and what long-term results did the punishment cause?

4. Describe Nick's relationship with his father from childhood to adulthood.

5. What does Mrs. Lorenzo do for Nick? What is her motivation?

Chapter 3

1. How do Nick and Sara meet?

2. What is the "coincidence" that Sara learns about their future?

3. Describe their first year of marriage.

4. What causes Sara to become angry with Nick?

5. What was the "unwelcome news," and how did Nick and Sara react to it? What was Beth's reaction and "solution?"

6. What was the result, and how did the couple deal with it, both together and individually?

Chapter 4

1. With what physical malady is Sara dealing? How has it affected her marriage? Her life?

2. What does Emma offer to do for Sara? Why was Sara surprised by the offer?

3. For what recommendation does Sara ask Emma?

4. How does Sara answer her question?

5. Why did Sara think she was a Christian?

6. What did Emma show Sara in the Bible?

7. How did Emma help Sara?

8. What happened after Sara prayed?

Chapter 5

1. Who is Steve, and what is his relationship to Nick?

2. Why is Steve quitting his job? How does Nick respond to it?

3. What does Steve tell Nick about Jesus Christ?

4. Do you believe the message Steve shared with Nick? What does Nick do with what he has heard? What have you done with this news about Christ?

5. What is the couple's new journey, and what are their old problems?

6. What has happened with Sara's migraine headaches?

Chapter 6

1. Why hasn't Sara been able to make her marriage better?

2. What sounds scary to Sara?

3. What does Dr. Campbell ask Sara that causes her to be afraid? What do you believe caused her panic attack?

4. How did Sara feel about herself when she was at school? At home?

5. What was Sara's responsibility for what happened to her in the basement?

6. What is your definition of brokenness? Of surrender?

7. What did Dr. Campbell tell Sara she needed to give to God? What do you need to give to God?

8. Why did God save Sara? You? What does "saved" mean to you?

9. What do we need to do in order for God to accept us?

Chapter 7

1. Describe the immediate fruit of brokenness in Sara's life. How did it affect Nick?

2. For what does Sara ask Nick? What is his answer?

3. Where has the love gone in their marriage? What reasons would you give for what has happened?

4. What does Dr. Campbell mean by "the other side of the cross?"

5. Who was Sara's "old man?" Describe him.

6. If you have been born again by the Spirit of God, who was your "old man?" Describe him.

7. What happened to Sara when Jesus died on the cross? To you?

8. What did Sara surrender to God? What can you surrender?

9. Describe the prison inside Sara's heart. Is there anyone in your prison?

10. What happened to Sara's nightmare? Why?

Chapter 8

1. What parallel did Sara realize was between her father's and Nick's behavior?

2. How did each man make her feel?

3. What can happen to hurt feelings if not released to God?

4. What predominant feeling did Sara realize she was carrying? What was the basis for that feeling? What was the root of the hurt?

5. Are you carrying hurt feelings? What is their root? Can you accept the fact that hurt turns to anger when harbored in your heart? What would it take for you to surrender that to the Lord?

6. Does God consider your part in the equation, your anger, sin?

7. What was the effect of Sara's feelings of rejection, hurt, and anger in her life and marriage?

8. Describe the importance of Sara's letters. How did they help her?

9. For what did Sara need to forgive her father? Nick?

10. How could it be possible that Sara could treat Nick differently? Is there someone in your life that you wish you could treat differently? What might need to happen for that to become a reality?

11. What is your definition of forgiveness? What have you learned thus far about forgiveness?

12. Does forgiving someone mean the relationship will be restored? Why or why not?

13. How do anger, bitterness, and unforgiveness block God's love? Is there someone in your life toward whom your love is blocked? Who is it?

14. What is an arrow prayer? In what circumstances might you use it?

Chapter 9

1. How had Sara's forgiving Nick changed her attitude and behavior toward him?

2. How has the change in Sara affected Nick?

3. What sport do Nick and Dr. Campbell have in common?

4. Does Dr. Campbell promise Nick that his counseling will "fix" Sara? Why not?

5. What is the purpose of the counseling?

6. Who has the power to change Nick? How?

7. What made Nick come home? What was Sara's reaction?

8. Is there someone in your life who needs to come home? Someone you need to let back into your life? Who is it?

9. Describe Nick's relationship with his father. His mother.

10. Who in Nick's life is like his mother?

11. What kinds of emotions took place in Nick's childhood home? In yours?

12. How had Nick felt about the many moves he asked his family to make? How is his opinion of those moves changing? How is your opinion changing about some of

the things you've done in your life? Are there things you thought were okay and you now realize might have hurt or affected someone close to you negatively? What are they?

13. To whom did Nick write his letter of forgiveness? What was the major thing for which he forgave him?

Chapter 10

1. Describe Sara's relationship with Jane.

2. Whom does Jane hate, and how did that affect Sara's life?

3. What favor does Jane ask of Sara?

4. What is Jane's illness, and what happens to her?

5. How many times does death knock?

6. What is Jane's condition after the second stroke?

7. What does Sara know she must do before her sister dies?

8. Describe what Sara does for her sister in the hospital room.

9. Who come to see Jane before she dies?

10. When death knocks the third time, what happens to Jane?

Chapter 11

1. What is Sara's new career?

2. Why did she choose it?

Chapter 12

1. What is Sara's connection to Andrea?

2. What event makes Andrea leave her childhood home?

3. Who is Mr. Riley, and how did his actions affect Andrea's life?

4. What did her new manager do, and how did that affect her? What is Andrea's opinion of men?

5. Who is Tony Scott? Describe him.

6. What is his opinion of parenthood? Why?

7. Why did Andrea leave Tony?

8. Where does she go, and what changes does she find when she arrives?

9. Why does Andrea blame herself for Josh's death? Describe her flashback.

10. What does Andrea learn upon her visit to her parents' church?

Chapter 13

1. What is Proclaim Recovery?

2. With what step does Andrea struggle? Why?

3. How do Andrea and Sara become linked?

4. What is Christ-centered counseling? Could it be different from just going to a counselor who is a Christian?

5. What is blocking Andrea's ability to forgive?

6. What happened to Andrea's old self?

7. Describe Andrea and Tony's new beginning.

Chapter 14

1. How is Andrea set free?

2. Describe the process Andrea must go through to be set free.

3. For what does she need to forgive Joshua? How did she feel about his deed?

4. How did her feelings develop into her own sin? What did she need to do with her sin?

Epilogue

1. What are the results of forgiveness in Sara's life and family? How does Sara go on to have an effect upon other people's lives?

2. What have you learned from reading this book? Has it helped you in any way, and if so, how has it helped?

Appendix B

Steps to Restoring Relationships

Our lives are comprised of relationships. *Webster* says that a relationship is the way in which two people talk to, behave toward, and deal with each other, or the way in which two or more people or things are connected. There are many circumstances which spawn relationships, from our nuclear family to our work and play environments.

What are the ingredients for a healthy relationship? For it to be healthy, there must be a respect for each other and an acceptance of the individual as God has created him. But many are involved in unhealthy ones. So, what causes relationships to tear apart?

1. A relationship begins to die when one of the pair tries to control the other's behavior, essentially trying to remake the person in his own image. Do you agree or disagree with this?

2. What one perceives as rejection from another can cause internalized hurt feelings developing into anger and unforgiveness. There are two kinds of rejection, overt and covert. Examples of overt are things like a parent leaving his spouse and children. Covert is a parent wishing his little girl had been born a boy and not accepting his daughter. Can you think of other examples of both covert, hidden, and overt, open and obvious rejection?

What Is the Normal Response to a Perceived Loss or Hurt?

A loss or hurt usually gives rise to anger. Because anger is at the root of all injustice and the wrongs done to mankind, it is beneficial to understand what it is.

Anger is an emotional response to a blocked goal, a hurt, or a perceived loss.

Anger begins with a blocked goal, or a loss or injury of some kind.

It can be the:

- loss of a desired goal
- loss of self-esteem
- loss of a possession
- loss of an ability or talent
- loss of a relationship
- etc.

When a hurt takes place, look for the anger trail.

The Anger Trail

HURT -------*turns into*-------- **ANGER**
BITTERNESS
UNFORGIVENESS
EVENTUALLY MURDER OR
MURDEROUS THOUGHTS OR
FEELINGS

How do we usually deal with hurt feelings in our lives?

1. Ignore them—It didn't happen.
2. Try to forget about them.

167

3. Become angry with the person.
4. Put up a wall between me and the person.
5. Ignore the person who caused them.
6. Develop and hold unforgiveness towards him, excusing myself from confronting the problem.
7. Sever the relationship.

What is the Biblical answer to our hurt?

He was despised and rejected by men; a man of sorrows, and acquainted with grief; and as one from whom men hide their faces he was despised and we esteemed him not. Surely he has borne our griefs and carried our sorrows (Isa. 53:3).

Jesus endured the most extreme rejection from those he came to save. There is nothing that has or can happen to me that Jesus has not experienced.

There is no temptation overtaken me except that is common to man (1 Cor. 10:13).

And being found in human form, he humbled himself by becoming obedient to the point of death, even death on a cross (Phil. 2:8).

I have been crucified with Christ. It is no longer I who live, but Christ who lives in me. And the life I now live in the flesh I live by faith in the Son of God, who loved me and gave himself for me (Gal. 2:20).

Explanation: The *I* who was crucified is the man I was before Christ saved me. That *I* no longer lives, but now the life I now live in this body is the life of Christ in and through me as I learn to live by faith in him.

Living by faith means that I accept *all things* that come into my life as first coming through his hand for my good, including hurts and rejections.

And we know that for those who love God all things work together for good, for those who are called according to his purpose (Rom. 8:28).

For those whom he foreknew he also predestined to be conformed to the image of his Son (Rom. 8:29a).

Our being conformed to Christ means that we *will* be rejected, and we trust Christ in us to handle that rejection.

People will reject us in this world, because they are also sinners and imperfect people. We must not look to others for our love and acceptance, for only One can love and accept us perfectly.

Just as He chose us in Him before the foundation of the world, that we should be holy and without blame before Him in love, having predestined us to adoption as sons by Jesus Christ to Himself, according to the good pleasure of His will, to the praise of the glory of His grace, by which He made us accepted in the Beloved (Eph. 1:4–6, NKJV).

Because God chose us, predestined us to be adopted as sons by Jesus Christ, we are totally accepted because we are in the Beloved, who is Jesus Christ. That's it. We are accepted, not because of anything we do, but because we are in Christ. That must be enough. I am accepted by God because I am in Christ. The God of the universe accepts me in Christ, not based upon my worth, but His worth.

On a scale of 1–10, how accepted is Jesus Christ to his Heavenly Father? He's a 10. So, how accepted am I to my Heavenly Father? I'm a 10 because *my life is hidden with Christ in God* (Col. 3:3).

We come into this world looking for love and acceptance. In a perfect world, we receive them from our parents and family, but if those needs are not met, we develop patterns of behavior that will try to gain love and acceptance. We become performers, doing what others want to earn their acceptance. That only lasts for a while, and we work harder and harder to feel loved, often to our detriment. We work so others will love and accept us, and we work for our own self-acceptance. I become like a hamster on a wheel, running faster and faster.

God wants us to accept his unconditional love that he gave us in the person of Jesus Christ, who loved us sacrificially, in spite of our sin and rebellion. We don't have to perform for his love. He loves us because that's who he is.

Beloved, let us love one another, for love is from God, and whoever loves has been born of God and knows God. Anyone who does not love does not know God, because God is love (1 John 4:7–8).

Anger

Anger is a God-given emotion that serves as a response mechanism of the soul to an event or circumstance in the moment. It is a normal, valid emotion, which becomes a problem when it goes unresolved.

Wrong ways to handle anger:

1. Suppress it. Anger turned inward results in depression.
2. Deny it. Most of us would rather die than admit we are angry.

3. Blame others. This relieves us of the responsibility for our anger.
4. Stay angry/hold a grudge. Some get angry and stay angry for years.

Handling Anger Correctly

Admit that you are angry. Own it as yours and take responsibility for it. It is the product of your indwelling sin.

Be honest before God. We need to ask God to reveal what is really causing the anger. We need to remember that our flesh wants things to go our way, and we don't like it when they don't. Don't let yourself do a slow burn on any issue. Jesus is your strength. *My grace is sufficient for you, for my power is made perfect in weakness* (2 Cor. 12:9). We can appropriate him as our strength to handle the situation.

God's Provision for Resolving Anger

Be kind to one another, tenderhearted, forgiving one another, as God in Christ forgave you (Eph. 4:32).

Until forgiveness is a settled issue, you won't realize your identity in Christ and live out of his life within. God's solution for anger is to forgive. We are to forgive others in the same way that he forgave us. What does it mean to forgive? What exactly did God do? How did He forgive us? For whose sin did He die? What happened to the sin of the person who wronged or hurt you?

Aspects of Forgiveness

In Matthew 18:21–35, Jesus spoke of important aspects of forgiveness. It is a gift we do not deserve. *Then Peter came up and said to him, Lord, how often will my brother sin against me, and I forgive him? As many as seven times? Jesus said to him, I do not say to you seven times, but seventy-seven times* (Matt. 18:21–22). Please read the entire passage.

- It is erasing or forgiving what is due, canceling the debt owed, and giving up all claims.
- Once received from God, it is to be passed on to others.
- Unforgiveness results in personal torture and inner torment.

> *Then his master summoned him and said to him, "You wicked servant! I forgave you all that debt because you pleaded with me. And should not you have had mercy on your fellow servant, as I had mercy on you?" And in anger his master delivered him to the jailers, until he should pay all his debt. So also my heavenly Father will do to every one of you, if you do not forgive your brother from your heart* (Matt. 18:32–35).

In your own life, who might your jailers be?

Reasons Why I Would Choose to Forgive

Paul spent the first three chapters of Ephesians telling us who we are in Christ as the basis for forgiving others. God's forgiveness of me makes me a forgiver of others. Read those chapters and write down what it says about who you now are as a believer.

1. *His divine power has granted to us all things that pertain to life and godliness, through the knowledge of him who called us to his own glory and excellence, by which he has granted to us his precious and very great promises, so that through them you may become partakers of the*

divine nature, having escaped from the corruption that is in the world because of sinful desire (2 Pet. 1:3–4). I am a partaker of the divine nature. My new nature in Christ is that I am forgiving. As a forgiven person in Christ, I have been made a forgiver of others. I make a choice to forgive based upon who I am in Christ. It's the way I was designed to deal with hurts and losses. If I focus on my emotions, then my soul becomes preoccupied with losses.

2. Forgiving frees my soul to live in the moment and express Christ's life. I am not designed to carry the burden of losses and hurts.

    Let us lay aside every encumbrance and the sin which so easily entangles us and let us run with endurance the race that is set before us, fixing our eyes on Jesus, the author and perfecter of our faith, who for the joy set before him endured the cross, despising the shame, and has sat down at the right hand of the throne of God. For consider him who has endured such hostility by sinners against himself, so that you will not grow weary and lose heart (Heb. 12:1–3).

3. Forgiveness frees me up to receive from others. *There is no fear in love, but perfect love casts out fear, because fear involves punishment (torment), and the one who fears is not perfected in love. We love, because He first loved us* (1 John 4:18–19).

4. My basic needs are met in Christ. Not all my wants and expectations, but my essential needs, those things without which I cannot live, are met in Christ.

    For in him all the fullness of Deity dwells in bodily form, and in him you have been made complete (Col. 2:9–10).

Forgiveness is a *decision*, a *choice*, based on an *act of the will* (not a feeling), done by faith before God, in which we give up our right to hold another person accountable for the wrong he has done to us. This choice is now made rationally because, not only has God forgiven me totally, but he also has made me a new person—a forgiving person with the forgiving life of Jesus inside me.

> *Forgiveness is agreeing to live with the*
> *consequences of another person's sin.*

Forgiveness is costly. We pay the price for the evil we forgive. Yet, we are going to live with those consequences whether we want to or not. The choice here is whether we're going to live with them in the bitterness of unforgiveness or the freedom of forgiveness.

Jesus forgave by taking the consequences of our sin upon himself. In true forgiveness, the offended party absorbs or bears the penalty of the other person's sin. We forgive because God forgave us, and we release our unforgiveness, our anger, and the offender's sin to God.

Forgiveness includes:

1. Charging the debt by acknowledging the hurt. (Be specific).
   Charging the emotional debt.
   Acknowledging the debt (How did it make me feel?).
   Calculating the cost (See Calculating Hurts Worksheet, Appendix C).

2. Canceling the debt.
   Releasing the person from the debt he owes me, saying, in effect, he never has to make it up to me or pay me back. "You are now free. You are forgiven. I release you, and I place you in the hands of Jesus Christ." I accept

the person unconditionally, just as he is, and I release the person of the responsibility to make me feel loved and accepted. I look to Jesus alone to meet my need for security and significance. I accept that I might be hurt again.

3. Walking in Forgiveness
    Standing by my decision to forgive means that I remember the event of forgiveness, not the offense. I choose, by an act of my will, to keep my accounts at 0, which means forgiving any additional offenses.

Whom Might I Need to Forgive?

1) Forgiving Myself

Is forgiving myself like playing God? It is important to remember that we are dealing with anger stemming from false expectations for ourselves. When we forgive ourselves, we are simply accepting and agreeing with God's forgiveness of us. Often people beat themselves up for sins God has already forgiven. Playing judge, jury, and warden in our own life is more like playing God than choosing to accept his forgiveness. Many people find it easier to connect with their anger toward themselves by saying to God, "I forgive myself for—.

2) Forgiving God

Is it right to forgive God? Technically, God does not need our forgiveness, for he cannot do anything wrong. In forgiving God, we are dealing with our bitterness and anger toward him for what we may perceive he withheld, or something he gave that may have caused pain. Our anger toward God is based upon what we perceive he should or should not have done. What we are actually doing is being honest about the disappointment and pain we feel in our relationship with God. This is very important to recognize and deal with in this forgiveness step. Though Job clung to God throughout his ordeal and was emotionally honest with him all along, the breakthrough for Job came with his repenting of his demanding spirit and letting God be God. (See Job 42:1–6). Whenever possible, I encourage people to use the correct terminology as they pray to forgive God. "God, I forgive you for ..." The attitude of the heart is the critical issue.

3) Forgiving Others

Why should I forgive someone who hasn't repented of his or her sin? Won't doing so just lead to more hurt? Forgiveness is not for the benefit of the perpetrator, although he might benefit from it, and it could pave the way for reconciliation and restoration at a later time. Forgiveness is a crucial element in resolving anger and bitterness toward others. It is necessary in order to experience Christ as your life. As we choose to forgive, emotional honesty is absolutely necessary in order to forgive from the heart and experience emotional healing.

What is the deepest hurt(s) you have experienced in life? By whom? Maybe this is an ongoing thing in your life. Who is the person(s) who causes your heart to start pounding the moment you see them? Use the space below to write your answer.

Reasons Why We Don't Forgive

Reasons are followed by the truth in quotations.

1. Pride. Forgiving someone makes me look weak. I want to feel better than others. I want to be strong and superior. If I'm right, then I don't have to give in. "But pride is what keeps me in bondage and hinders growth."
2. I don't want to give up my excuse-making system, (my coping mechanisms/my flesh). "At first, freedom can be scary. I am out of my comfort zone. I will be learning a whole new way of living if I learn to forgive."
3. If I were to forgive, I would feel out of control. I want to feel in control and be able to manipulate others by holding the debt against them. "The truth is I am out of control when I cling to my hurt and anger. I am the one in bondage."
4. If I forgive, I may get hurt again. "The truth is I am going to get hurt again by others regardless of what I do. So the issue is, what is the best response to these upcoming hurts so that I am not living in fear and being controlled by others? When I hold onto the hurt, I am in fact allowing the other person to control me."
5. If I ignore it, the problem will go away. "The problem just gets buried and resurfaces later. Unresolved baggage from the past is brought into the present."
6. Revenge. The person *has* to pay for it. He needs to be punished and learn a lesson. I want to hang on to the right to be the judge. "I am not God, and trying to play God will get me into trouble. Vengeance belongs to the Lord."
7. Failure to understand God's love and forgiveness for me. "I cannot give a gift to someone unless I first have something to give."

8. Failure to forgive myself. Before I can truly forgive others I must forgive myself. "I can only love my neighbor to the degree I love myself."

9. It seems too easy and unfair. It seems I'm overlooking or condoning their sin. "No, in fact I am charging and documenting the debt and recognizing that Jesus died on the cross for that sin."

10. I should wait for the person to come to me first. "It rarely happens."

11. The person isn't sorry for what he's done. "Chances are he'll never be sorry. Forgiveness is primarily for my benefit. I don't need to wait."

12. If I choose to forgive, I'm acting like a hypocrite because I don't "feel" loving and forgiving. "The truth is, I'm a hypocrite if I don't forgive because my real nature in Christ is now a forgiving nature, if indeed his Holy Spirit lives in me."

13. I must wait for a convenient time and a "feeling." "It will never be convenient. I will never 'feel' like forgiving. Forgiveness is a choice, an act of my will, not a feeling. Jesus never told us to wait until we 'feel' like forgiving before we forgive. He told us to forgive because he forgave us on the cross."

14. Thinking it takes too much time. I don't have time to forgive. "Really? I can't afford not to forgive. I am the one in torment and suffering."

15. I am afraid of feelings that might be stirred up. "God knows how to gently get out the feelings that need to be healed. I won't die or go crazy. He will take care of me."

Common Misconceptions Regarding Forgiveness

I feel like I have forgiven because:

- I don't feel angry anymore. Forgiveness is not about not feeling angry anymore.
- I am able to *justify and explain* this person's hurtful behavior. I can see some of the reasons he or she did it.
- I am able to separate the person from his behavior. Forgiveness is being able to say "what a person does and who he is are two different things."
- I am giving him the benefit of the doubt. He didn't mean it. Forgiveness says no one is perfect, so you need to cut people some slack.
- I am saying to myself, "Time heals all wounds." I am willing to be patient and just go on with my life. Forgiveness is a process that takes a lot of time. Time heals nothing. Forgiveness heals the soul.
- I am willing to forget about it. Forgiving is forgetting. It is saying, "Let's just forget about it."
- I am able to pray for the person who has hurt me.
- I have asked God to forgive them.
- I have asked them to forgive me.
- I am waiting for them to come to me to ask for forgiveness. Once they do this, I will forgive them. I am willing to forgive.
- I have confronted this person about his behavior.
- I am able to say that I haven't really been hurt that badly. I just pretend that the hurt was really not that big of a thing.
- I am able to act as if it never happened.
- I have attempted reconciliation. Forgiveness says that the broken relationship must be restored.
- I am willing.

How to Forgive

1. Using the Calculating Hurts Worksheet in Appendix C, first pray and ask God to show you the names of each person who has hurt you and toward whom you hold anger and unforgiveness. Use a separate sheet for each person. Pray Psalm 139:23–24: "Search me, O God, and know my heart; test me and know my thoughts. Point out anything in me that offends you, and lead me along the path of everlasting life."

2. Write the person's name at the top of the Calculating Hurts Worksheet, and then proceed to fill in the columns: The Offense (Event or Behavior that Hurt Me Deeply); The Debt from the Injury (How It Made Me Feel); Expectation (What I Had Hoped For).

3. After completing your first sheet, take what you have written and picture Jesus Christ standing in front of you in his flowing white robes. Before proceeding, pray this prayer. "Dear Lord Jesus, please give me your grace to release my anger and unforgiveness toward ____. I know I am your child and you live inside me. Work a deep forgiveness in me so I can let go of the past."

4. Picture the person whose name you have written on the worksheet. Take him by the hand and stand before Jesus. Begin to talk to the person. You might begin like this: "Dad, when you didn't pay any attention to me when I was growing up, it hurt me deeply. It made me feel unloved and unimportant." Continue on, putting into words every emotion you have held inside. Don't hold anything back. It's important to get out everything you've stuffed, even if you think it's irrational. Your feelings belong to you, and they have translated into beliefs about yourself.

5. Now turn to Jesus Christ who stands before you. Pray this prayer. "Dear Lord Jesus, I have been angry with ____

for a long time, and I have held unforgiveness toward him. I now reach into my heart and take out the jar of black sludge, my sin of anger, hatred, unforgiveness, and I put it in your hands. I ask you to forgive me for my sin. I now turn to _____ and offer him my forgiveness. Jesus, you are the forgiver, the one who died for me so I can be forgiven of my sins. Please forgive through me."

"Dad, I choose by an act of my will to forgive you. I cancel the debt that I have held against you for most of my life, and I set you free. I give up all my expectations of you, and I tell you that you don't owe me anything to pay the debt. Jesus has paid my debts and yours. I know that I have kept you in a prison cell in my heart, and so now I reach down and unlock the door of the prison and set you free. I release you into the hands of God, and I give him permission to work in your life however he sees fit."

Picture in your mind your unlocking the jail cell and letting him go free. Jesus will be there with you, and he will do this work of forgiveness for you and in you. Some people have seen Jesus take the offender and walk away with him, leaving the praying person free of him. There might be a sense of relief, as if a great boulder has been lifted from your shoulders. Whether you feel anything or not, know that you have received forgiveness for your anger and unforgiveness, and you have canceled the debt against the one you have held in the vise of unforgiveness.

Continue filling out a Calculating Hurts Worksheet for each person God has brought to your mind. This might take you some time. Don't rush it. It's important that all hurt, anger, and unforgiveness is released. For each person you hold prisoner with unforgiveness, there is a jar of black sludge, sin, towards that person. It's your part that has happened in your heart as a result of the offense against you. This is very important to clean out for you to be free and for forgiveness to be complete. Forgiveness is not only canceling the debt that you believe another owes you, it is also dealing with the sin that has grown in your heart towards the offender. Both parts are necessary in order for the process to be complete.

Complete the process for each offender by walking through the steps outlined above. Forgiveness is freedom, and Jesus Christ is its author. He came so that we may have his life living inside us to give us the power to forgive others.

When you have worked through every Calculating Hurts Worksheet and have forgiven each person, you now have a model of forgiveness to use for the rest of your life. Whenever an offense occurs, or you have a difficulty in a relationship, you can go to God and release the offense before it develops into unforgiveness. We can keep short accounts with God, giving up our expectations of others and releasing our control of how we think others should behave.

God is in control, and we experience freedom when we can let him be God. We are not God, and we cannot control other people, what they say and what they do. Release others into God's hands, and admit that he is God and you're not. Set yourself and others free by forgiving and letting God be in charge. He is and always will be. Amen.

Appendix C

Calculating Hurts Worksheet

Offender: _____

The Offense Event or Behavior That Hurt Me Deeply	The Debt from the Injury How It Made Me Feel	Expectation What I Had Hoped For

About the Author

Joyce C. Stanley received a B.A. from Penn State University, an M.Ed. from State University of New York, and certification from Exchanged Life Ministries Colorado to counsel and train others in biblical counseling. She began counseling in Houston, Texas, in 1984 and in 1995 founded, along with her husband John, Exchanged Life Ministries, Southeast Texas. From 1995 through 2008, Joyce counseled from a Christ-centered, grace-life perspective untold numbers of individuals struggling with life's circumstances.

After moving to the Dallas metroplex, Joyce currently counsels those experiencing depression and broken relationships. She teaches a community-wide workshop dealing with anger, unforgiveness, and the resultant fractured families, based on the information in *It's Not Too Late.*

As a member of Network 220, an organization of exchanged life offices across America, Joyce functions as a mentor and advisor to others whom the Stanleys' ministry has trained to carry on the work begun in Houston.

Joyce has been married to her college sweetheart John for fifty years. She is the proud mother of one son, Douglas, and a very involved grandmother of four beautiful granddaughters.

CPSIA information can be obtained
at www.ICGtesting.com
Printed in the USA
LVHW051755010623
748479LV00002B/262